Small Talk About Big Deals

PREFACE

Edwin H. Kennedy, born in Utrecht, the Netherlands, didn't exactly have a smooth ride through youth and school. He fought his way through and, like so many looking for a sense of purpose, found himself in the Military Intelligence Service at a young age.

It was there that he caught the bug for technology, habit-breaking, and flipping conventional wisdom on its head. When an IT company dangled the bait to kickstart his career, the psychological tests all pointed to one thing: this guy was born for commerce. He took that talent and ran with it, co-developing a Fraud Analysis System for Banks that got the attention of a major American outfit in Texas. They wanted him to build their Financial Industry Group from scratch—no small feat, but Edwin was never one to shy away from a challenge.

Then life threw him a curveball—family changes that made him rethink his priorities. So, he did what most wouldn't dare: he walked away from the corporate grind and chased what really set his soul on fire—growth. His journey took him across continents, working with companies in Europe, India, The Caribbean, and the USA, where he stumbled upon his second great love: cultures. During an MBA program, he found what felt like the missing piece: the power of sharing knowledge.

Edwin poured these passions into his company, SalesPulse, a beast of a business dedicated to driving the growth of international companies. He'll tell you he's almost egoless—an interesting claim in the world of commerce—because, in his mind, it's all about collaboration and connecting with like-minded souls. The motto? "Grow together."

Then there's Kate Yandoh Harris, from New York, USA, who was his English teacher back in the day when they were both just starting out.

After living and teaching English in the Netherlands and Belgium, Kate returned to her home country to work for The Coca-Cola Company, where she wrote speeches for the CEO and other executives. An early adopter of social media and content marketing, she learned to inventively capture attention and develop international markets for tourism, before her curiosity took her to the tech sector to help nonprofits amplify their impact using digital marketing and AI. She has served numerous arts organizations as a Board member, marketer, and occasional performer in plays, musicals, and band battles.

They kept in touch over the years, trading insights on culture, careers, and the twisted landscape of politics.

Together, they bring you this book, Small Talk About Big Deals, their shot at bridging cultures by opening people's eyes to a simple truth: there's your opinion, there's my opinion, and somewhere in between, there's reality.

SMALL TALK ABOUT BIG DEALS

TABLE OF CONTENTS

92
L.E.S
BOWERY
NEW YORK

MY WHY AND HOW IT DISAPPEARED

REMEMBERING AARON AND MOVING FORWARD

It's been almost three years since we lost our youngest son, Aaron Elijah. Putting the impact of such a loss into words feels nearly impossible. Aaron wasn't just our child; he was our muse, our joy, the light that guided our every step forward.

Even now, so many kind souls ask about Aaron, and it feels only right to create a space for him in this book.

Sharing knowledge and learning from each other has always been a huge part of my life. But, after this loss, it proved to be essential to building back a different life. To reach and possibly help more people on a broader, international stage, I went to work on this book with the help of my brilliant American friend, Kate Yandoh Harris.

Life Revolving Around Aaron

Every decision I made, every future plan I envisioned, was built around the idea of Aaron living a long and happy life. We began to sense this shift when Aaron was around two years old. He wasn't developing like his older brother, Joshua. Aaron was heavier, despite a normal diet, struggled with speech, and seemed deeply absorbed in his own world. After a long journey of searching, we learned he had Sotos syndrome. Aaron grew into a big, gentle young man, facing challenges with his metabolism, speech, movement, and cognition. Later, severe autism and epilepsy joined the mix.

From the moment Aaron's condition became clear, we restructured our family life around him. I put plans to move abroad on hold, and left a job I loved that required constant travel. Our first priority was to understand Aaron's challenges and figure out how to support him. Only then could my career come back into focus. This way, Aaron could always be home. It was hard at times, but we never regretted it. The love we experienced was immense, and we all came to value the importance of caring for each other.

An old colleague, knowing our situation, reached out with an opportunity that would allow me to work closer to home. It was the right choice, especially when we received confirmation that Aaron would live with significant mental and physical limitations.

A Shift in Focus

In the years that followed, I dove into interim work, focusing on boosting commercial departments in various companies. It was something I loved, something I was good at, and it allowed me to plan for Aaron's future. Over the years, I've worked with numerous companies on growth, change, improvement, and innovation—work that continues to bring me joy every day.

When our eldest son Joshua showed an entrepreneurial spirit, I started several ventures with him, hoping he could one day help care for his brother. When Aaron passed away in 2021, my career's "why" vanished too. I took time to rediscover it. Right after his death, I completed a takeover assignment and spent a year in advisory roles, guiding entrepreneurs.

This allowed me to step back from heavy responsibilities, heal, and find a new path with my wife. It worked well, and now I run my own company, SalesPulse, with great satisfaction. Currently I am the Interim Director for a large organisation, hold interests in several companies, write a book, and mentor entrepreneurs in their growth. SalesPulse is evolving into a collective, with my partner Roy and strong allies in communication, marketing, lead generation, finance, mergers & acquisitions, and legal.

Honoring Aaron

I believe we've found a way to give Aaron's loss a meaningful place in our lives, holding his memory close even as we ache from missing him. I'm now more aware than ever of the importance of friendship, camaraderie, love, and respect. I've been initiated as an Apprentice Freemason, drawing deep knowledge and brotherhood from this circle.

Through my work with Stichting Papageno, I can give back to people like Aaron. As a volunteer at nlgroeit, I help young entrepreneurs realize their ambitions.

Gratitude and Inspiration

In the past two years, family, friends, colleagues, and acquaintances have shown me what truly matters: being there when needed and staying longer than expected. Thank you for that.

To every reader with an idea, dream, or goal I can help with: please reach out. I welcome the chance to be of service because if there's one thing I've learned this past year, it's that helping others ultimately helps you too.

Aaron's memory lives on in everything we do. His presence continues to inspire us to strive for a better future, both for ourselves and for others. Through giving and sharing, we honor his life and his legacy.

LET'S GROW!

My name is Edwin Kennedy, and I'm a Growth Guide. My focus is always forward—constantly anticipating the next steps, imagining different scenarios, and keeping my sights set on that distant point on the horizon.

The past? It's a teacher, nothing more. I learn from it, but I don't linger there. I try to enjoy the present, but any celebration is brief. Success is a moment, and then it's time to move on. "Onward," as I like to say.

Most of my clients have a lot in common: they're young, they launched their businesses early, and they've hit impressive milestones. But here's the thing—they often think that a brilliant product will just sell itself. They miss the mark on empathy, which would help them connect better with their audience.

When we first meet, there's usually mutual interest, but it's not quite the right time to dive into collaboration (I'll explain more in Chapter, 'Understand the Three Phases').

After a few meetings, the frustration starts to surface. They've been successful, but now they're stuck. What used to work isn't cutting it anymore, and they want more. That's when the door opens for real collaboration—where we start sharing visions, insights, and experiences.

No judgment.

It's like a gathering of Freemasons—everyone's there to share, to learn, not to prove who's right.

Almost every potential client or partner asks me the same thing: "What do you actually do to achieve growth, and what's your secret?"

Let me bust that myth right away: there's no secret, and there are no guarantees. But what I bring is experience, and a deep passion for aiming high.

Mix that with a respect for process and discipline, an ability to read people, the understanding that any decision is better than no decision, and a genuine love for what I do, and you'll get a pretty good idea of how I work with my clients.

We take a dream, turn it into a tangible goal, assess where we're at, and craft strategies and tactics fueled by passion and the resources at hand.

And there's one thing we always keep front and center: the Line-Up.

SIDE NOTE: What's In it for You?

It seemed like I'd stumbled into the most luxurious and interesting teaching job ever.

Fresh out of college, newly arrived in the Netherlands, and armed with an intensive Dutch course, I found myself teaching at a high-end language school.

My students? Executives, diplomats, and professionals who were smart, ambitious, and had very specific goals—leading international teams, navigating takeovers, delivering keynote presentations,
or closing big deals.

Forget the dull textbooks and worksheets. Instead, we took a conversation-based approach where they'd explain or role-play, and I'd pull out what they needed to practice or fine-tune.

What started as a language lesson quickly turned into an ongoing conversation about what really happens behind the scenes of business deals, along with a treasure trove of tips, tricks, hacks, and ideas for "changing the ground rules" when collaborating across cultures and personalities.

Edwin's stories about million-dollar deals, negotiating, selling, and communicating didn't just give us a ton of material for his sessions —they stayed with me and showed me how the approaches and mindsets that can effectively grow a business can serve you well in pursuit of other dreams.

We noticed that sometimes you need some structure to practice new ways of thinking, or to break out of ruts. So I've added some thought starters, exercises, and the occasional dose of a different perspective.

This book exists to spark growth in you. We hope that using some of the ideas and principles will help you with the things that are a 'big deal' in your life - personal and professional.

However you use it, you're doing it right!

-Kate

LIFE IN THE LINE-UP

Let's start with a dojo—a training place for martial arts like karate.

Walk into any dojo around the world, and you'll notice the same ritual. Everyone takes their place in the lineup. On the left, you'll find the beginners, perhaps just testing the waters. On the right, the seasoned practitioners stand with quiet confidence, their years of disciplined training etched into every movement.

At first glance, what seems to be a rigid hierarchy is actually a very level—and powerful—playing field.

When you first visit—maybe because you got a free session—you'll find yourself on the left, trying to follow those on the right. A few weeks pass, and then someone new joins the class. You're no longer the newest member, and that person looks to you for guidance.

That experienced practitioner on the far right might not be the strongest person in the room, but they've fought a thousand battles. They've honed their skills, not just in brute strength, but in the art of anticipation, moving with a grace that only comes from years of experience.

Now, think about your work life the same way. When you're just starting out, standing all the way to the left, it's easy to feel like everyone in the company is there to help you learn, to guide

"Martial Arts begins and ends with respect."
-Anko Itosu, father of modern-day karate

you through each step, with a pat on the back for every job well done.

As you move up, however, you gain more responsibility, face higher expectations, and receive less praise. This is where panic often sets in. It's the most terrifying place to be. The expectations are no longer as straightforward as when you were just beginning—now it feels like you have to know it all and do it all on your own.

When you finally make it to the far right, you have the opportunity to develop new ways of thinking and, above all, to keep learning. Because if you stop learning, eventually, you'll stagnate and destroy the progress you've made.

Here's the good news: every spot in the lineup offers a chance to grow—if you stay relentless about learning. Learn from those to your left, those to your right, and even those outside the dojo.

By being aware of and learning from everyone around you, you can ensure that you always have a place, even in a tech-driven world where change happens faster and faster, rendering old models of work and thinking obsolete.

See yourself in that lineup, but don't think: Ha, I'm much better than that beginner. And don't think: Oh no, I'm nowhere near the expert level. That's not the point of the lineup. It's about seeing yourself as part of a community, as part of a continuous growth process: Who can I learn from? And who can I teach? That's how you grow.

The great Confucius said, "In every art, the grandmasters were once students."

So, set your ego aside and embrace the opportunity to learn. Build relationships with the people to your left and right, but don't forget to look beyond your usual circle. There's always more out there to discover.

SIDE NOTE: The Dojo Is a Lot Like the Dance Floor

When I turned 30, I had a session with a well-known life coach who asked about my exercise regimen.

I proudly told her that I was an avid user of my apartment gym. Every morning, I would pound out an hour on the treadmill, elliptical, or stair climber—depending on which cardio punisher was available—always with music in my ears at full volume.

"What's going on in your mind while you're doing that?" she asked.

"Um…I'm seeing myself dancing in a music video or a musical or at the center of a big party…it keeps me from getting bored," I admitted.

"Have you ever considered signing up for a dance class and - just dancing in real life?"

I ended up booking a class through Emory University's continuing education program, mainly because I liked the sound of the teacher's name (Ofelia de La Valette, here's to you!). I've been on the dance floor ever since and can't imagine life without it.

Trying out karate and t'ai chi classes in the spirit of research confirmed that there is more overlap than you might think between the dojo and the dance floor - so, to grow using movement, you have ample options!

Grow from Your Place on the Floor: In dance, the more experienced dancers stand at the front. It's a sign of respect for their hard work and also an extra source of instruction and inspiration. If you're behind them, you find your spot in a 'dance window' between two dancers. They're not expected to move around to give you a better view of the mirror—they're focused on what's ahead, not who's coming up behind them.

Corrections Are a Gift: Whether the teacher is correcting one dancer or the whole group, you're expected to try out their tips. Getting singled out usually means you've caught their eye and have the potential to improve—not that you're a hopeless case. So say goodbye to that useless self-talk and hello to continuous improvement!

Face Fear (and Kick It to the Curb) with Practice: The dojo might have you confront fear by sparring and mastering techniques, but the dance floor throws a different challenge at you—facing something scarier than a fight in a dark alley: moving your body in front of an audience, maybe even performing. By practicing and repeating in a safe, non-judgmental space, you can train your body and mind to hit a sweet spot where you're free from other people's expectations!

Grow Faster with the Group: You tend to show up, you get inspired by those around you, you have the benefit of a guide, and you are highly likely to have more fun and a greater stress-busting benefit than if you were simply sweating solo.

"Dancing is simply moving your body... everyone can do it. It doesn't matter how high you can kick your leg; it doesn't matter what the shape or size of your body is. It doesn't matter if you have one leg or no legs; you can dance. Everybody has the ability to move some part of their body. Once you can move some part of your body, you can dance... I hate it when people say, 'Oh, I've got two left feet. I'm not a very good dancer. No, no, no, you are. If you're breathing, you're a good dancer."

Dr. Peter Lovatt

TRY THIS: Look Around (and Beyond) Your Lineup

Mapping Your Learning Line-Up

Think about the areas of your life where it's very clear you're part of a "learning line-up" (e.g., your job, a hobby, a skill you're developing). For each area, rate your position from 1 (absolute beginner/ thought this was a different class) to 10 (grandmaster/'Obi-Wan').

Now broaden your gaze. It's natural to focus on the people to your right, the classic mentors. But they aren't the only valuable sources of learning.

What about:
• **Peers in the Middle:** Likely facing similar challenges, so a natural source of empathy and practical solutions - and it may be easier to book regular time with them.

• **Up-and-Comers on the Left:** Here is an often overlooked source of ideas and growth: people new to the party in the sense of their age, experience, and time spent in this particular company. They are a great source of fresh perspectives and ideas from outside the usual.

• **Outside the Dojo:** The less like you they are, the more interesting. Who has lived a life that's the opposite of yours? Reaching outside the bubble can take effort, but it reaps rewards.

Bonus Exercise: Write a brief note of appreciation to someone in one of your "line-ups" who has helped you grow. This could be a mentor, a peer, someone you've taught...or even a 'difficult' person who challenged you.

WANDER OFF THE CAREER PATH

I'd say it's better not to want a career at all - but that's easy to say in hindsight.

When I was finishing school, the Netherlands still had compulsory military service, and I decided to get it over with right after high school. Believing you should do everything as well as possible, I signed up for a Commando or Marines training (the need for ... was already in me). To my surprise, I was called up for something completely different.

The tests showed I had a high analytical ability. On the intake day, I was put in a room with a handful of others and addressed by a top brass. We were selected for the Military Intelligence Service (some call it a contradiction in terms). Details would follow, but only after agreeing to further screening and placement at the SMID (School for Military Intelligence Service) and knowing we would have a schedule full of weekends and night shifts (spying doesn't stop at 5 pm on Fridays.) I called my dad for advice and decided to go for it.

I can't say much about it, but I never regretted that decision for a single day (lesson: your first instinct is (almost) always right.

After the training and some time to adjust, the schedule created a lot of paid time off, so I decided to register with a temp agency for some extra work and income. Since I could enter data into a computer system, It was a job as a secretary at a prominent French IT company. I managed to get in good with the woman who was supposed to show me the ropes, and just like that, I was working in IT!

A few months into the part-time work, I was called in by Jos, who turned out to be the company director. Jos had discovered my \schedule (after night duty in the military, I was in the office by 8 a.m., worked all day, used my paid time off to work another full day at the office, and then had evening duty the next day, allowing me to spend another full day at the office). Jos was impressed with my enthusiasm but wanted to protect me from myself.

He made me an offer I couldn't refuse: I could work on my days off, but not after night duty and not before evening duty. In return, I could spend that workday in the training center, and he would introduce me to his network once my military service was over. (Lesson: when a kind person wants to help you, don't overthink it and appreciate the offer. The real pros help wherever they can.) Jos kept his word. I completed my IT training, and after that, I had my pick of jobs—his network was eager to give me a chance.

Always keep your eyes open to future possibilities. Whether you're sticking with a steady job, exploring side gigs, or making smart investments, thinking ahead will prepare you for the inevitable shifts in the job market and your personal goals.

As life gets more complex, diversifying your professional life isn't just a safety net—it's a power move. It's how you take control, protect your financial future, and steer your career exactly where you want it to go.

TAKE THE LEAP – AND LEARN FROM IT

My boss, with a touch of humor, tasked me to "do something brilliant once a year." He even joked, "You can also do it twice, Edwin." It was a daunting yet exciting challenge. My mission was to generate revenue in the financial industry through outsourcing.

As I pondered this challenge, I remembered that in America, particularly in Dallas, Texas, there was an incredibly successful market for insurance outsourcing with EDS. This was surprising because insurers are typically conservative, yet they had embraced outsourcing there. I thought, if it works in Texas, where conservatism reigns, why can't it work here?

I approached my manager with a bold plan. "I want to go to Texas and learn from them," I said. He was skeptical but curious. "It's very different there," he pointed out. "Exactly," I replied. "That's why I want to go—to understand their culture and see how they think. I want to work with them, talk to them, and learn firsthand."

Speaking English was one thing, but communicating with cultural respect was another challenge altogether. Most people can order a hamburger in English, but understanding the nuances behind the language and connecting with people on a deeper level is much more complex. So, I sought out an American English coach to help me bridge this gap. This, if you recall from the beginning of this book, also led to its creation.

Armed with newfound linguistic and cultural understanding, I traveled to Texas. What I found there was a different world. The insurers in Dallas were conservative but open to innovative financial constructions. I realized that success here was not just about understanding the market but also about integrating into their way of thinking.

Back in the Netherlands, I applied what I had learned. I pitched the idea of smaller, manageable deals rather than massive, overwhelming ones. This revolutionary approach required convincing many people to shift their traditional business models. But it worked. We secured several small deals that eventually led to significant growth.

This experience taught me the importance of stepping out of my comfort zone and embracing new challenges. It reinforced the idea that doing something brilliant requires not just innovation but also a willingness to learn and adapt. By constantly challenging myself to think outside the box, I made significant strides in my career and inspired others to do the same.

Learning from Mistakes

It's easy to overlook or dismiss new ideas. If there's one piece of advice I could give anyone, it's this: if you really want something, go for it. Start a company. I've done it a couple of times. But remember, it's not all smooth sailing. Starting a company means taking on a lot of responsibility and dealing with inevitable setbacks. It's not about having a leased car every month, a fixed salary, or an easy path to getting a mortgage. Those comforts aren't guaranteed.

For example, people in my home country are praised simply for changing their winter tires on time. It's become such a routine. But, if you look at the bigger picture, this complacency leads to civilizations' decline. The Incas, the Chinese dynasties, the Turks, the Soviets, the Portuguese, the Spaniards, the English, and now the Americans—all have seen their power diminish because they took their dominance for granted.

Recognizing this can be freeing. It means understanding that where you are now isn't permanent. It's not something to be taken for granted. It's crucial to remember the English saying: "Never confuse motion with action." You need to do something substantial, not just go through the motions. Real change requires real action.

Admittedly, this is difficult. I struggle with it, too, but you have to try.

Curiosity fuels growth. It drives you to ask questions, seek new knowledge, and explore uncharted territories.

Why not embrace a restlessness that compels you to push boundaries and strive for more?

And...PS: The moment that you think you can do it alone, you are so screwed.

TRY THIS: Teach to Learn

If you really want to learn in a deep and lasting way, try the Feynman Method. Here's how to do it:

1. Explain the Concept: Start by explaining the concept as if you're teaching a child or a complete novice. Use simple language and avoid jargon. The goal is to break down the idea into its most basic parts so anyone can understand it.

2. Identify Gaps in Your Understanding: While you're explaining, take note of any areas where you struggle or rely on complex terms. These are likely gaps in your understanding. Go back to the source material to fill these gaps until you can explain everything clearly.

3. Refine and Simplify: Organize your explanation, simplifying it further where possible. As you review your notes, look for ways to make the explanation clearer and more concise. Regularly refine your notes to reinforce your understanding.

4. Test Your Understanding: Remember, if you can't explain something simply, you don't truly understand it. Revisit the concept periodically to ensure that your understanding remains strong.

Why This Works: The Feynman Method is named after Richard Feynman, a Nobel Prize-winning physicist known for his ability to explain complex topics in simple terms. By teaching others—or imagining you are—you force yourself to clarify your thoughts and identify areas where your understanding is shaky.

Additional Tip: To enhance your learning even further, try teaching the concept to someone else in real life. This could be a friend, a colleague, or online audience. Teaching others not only reinforces your own understanding but also helps you discover new perspectives and ideas.

Who Was Richard Feynman?

If you haven't met him yet, Richard Feynman was a ground-breaking scientist and Nobel laureate genius who played the bongo, wrote music and poetry, was heavily into cosplay, and led the investigation that uncovered the cause of the Challenger disaster. He was known not just for his brilliant mind but also for his ability to make science accessible and fun.

"I'm a Doctor, Jim, not a Rock Star"

"I'M A DOCTOR, JIM, NOT A ROCK STAR"

I often toss out the phrase—borrowed from Star Trek and famously echoed by Van Halen—when people invite me to speak at events. It's not about ego; it's about keeping it real.

I'm not in this game to dazzle with speeches. I've never been one for the limelight; I'm more about the substance. Sure, speeches have their place, but real change happens in the trenches, where you dig deep, get your hands dirty, and find the truth.

That's where the real value is—understanding people, getting into the weeds with their goals, and delivering the unvarnished truth like a Dutchman with no time for pleasantries. Sure, I can drop a few witty quotes (Oscar Wilde said it best: "The ability to quote is a serviceable substitute for wit"), but that's not the foundation you build a company on.

The people I work with are a special breed—sharp, successful, and young enough to still have fire in their bellies. They've built something real, often coming from a background where they had a brief stint with an employer, hated it, and jumped ship to start their own thing. Money wasn't their first love, but it followed them like an eager puppy.

And then, they hit the dreaded ceiling. Revenue, profit, growth—all stuck in a rut, like a broken record. They've tried bringing in help—a few colleagues, maybe even a commercial director or two—but the needle doesn't move.

The truly remarkable ones, though, are those who turn the mirror on themselves. They realize that part of the problem might be them. It's a humbling moment, and not everyone can handle it. But those who can find themselves at a crossroads. It's like Verne Harnish says in his Scaling Up model: every growth stage needs a different approach. Our savvy entrepreneurs get this—they're ready to look beyond the obvious.

At this point, they're not just listening; they're absorbing and questioning, and sometimes, they ask me to step in as a consigliere—a trusted advisor, a sounding board. This phase is golden: We start to click, blending two successful strategies, and before you know it, we've crafted the 2.0 version—refined, rejuvenated, and ready to break through that glass ceiling.

And yes, I do get on stage now and then, but I crave the back-and-forth with the audience. Sharing knowledge and experience that's what I do best. I'm not here to pull off miracles or be the star of the show. So, when I say, "I'm a doctor, not a rock star!" it's just my way of keeping things grounded.

I first noticed this approach sparked real interest when I started teaching sessions to MBA students. When they found out I wasn't just an academic but a real dealmaker who's closed millions of dollars in deals, worked with hot startups, and learned sales lessons hands-on, they started to wake up. Soon, we were having fun, passionate debates fueled by their curiosity.

The students wanted to know everything. They craved real stories and had loads of questions. Their curiosity was unfiltered (most were Dutch, like me—something we'll get into later).

After all, in the words of the great Anthony Bourdain, "Good food and good eating are about risk. And, if you don't take risks, you're destined to lead a dull, uninteresting life." The same goes for business—if you're unwilling to get uncomfortable, you're just going through the motions.

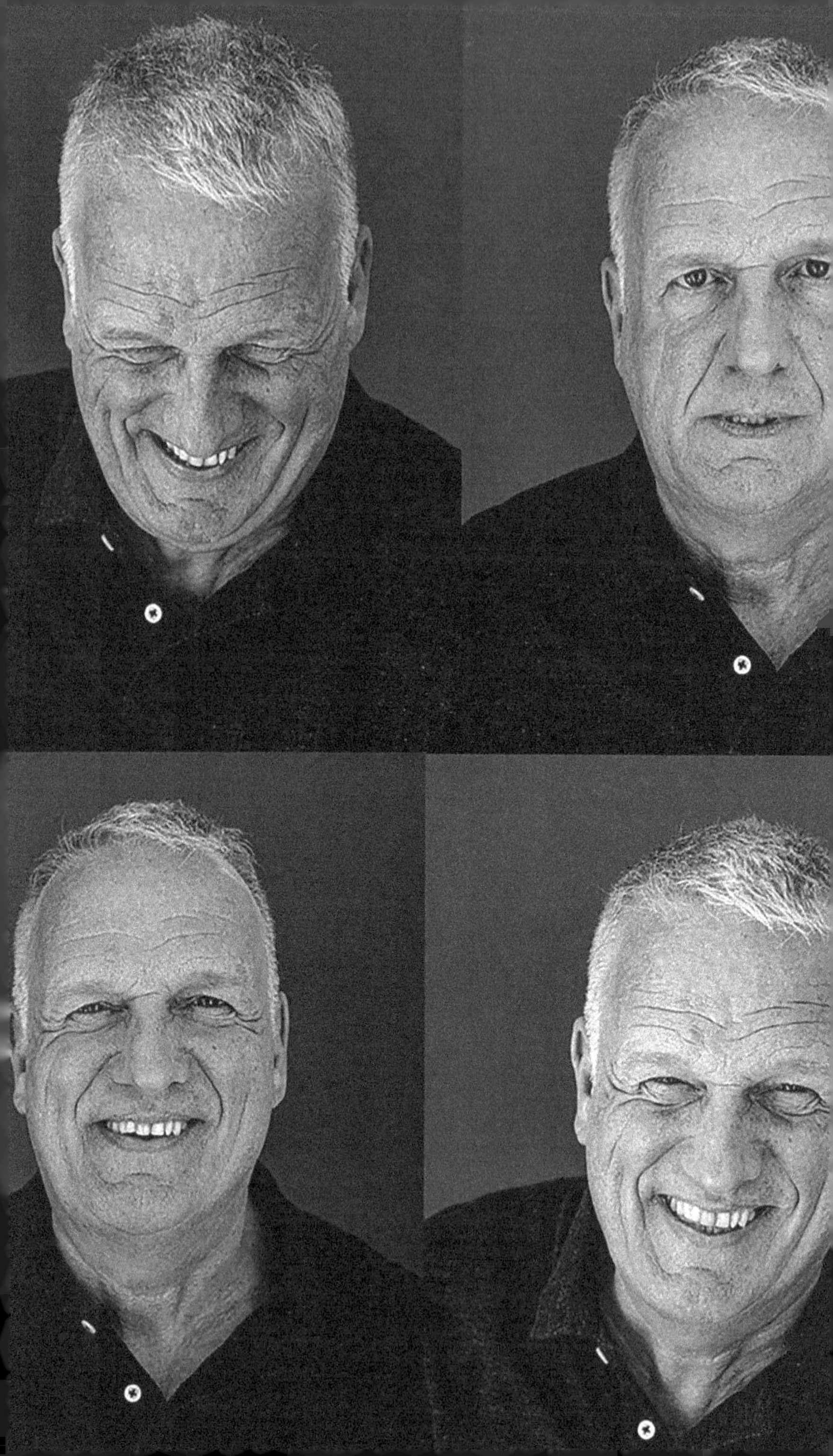

FIND YOUR FORM

Would you like a secret to success that's not really a secret?

Give form to who you are, what you offer, and what you're doing.

Do the work to truly understand what you want and the unique value you provide. Once you've defined that, you can spread this
clarity throughout your network, so people know exactly what you can do for them—and they'll call you when they need it.

Determining someone's "thing" is one of my favorite parts of a coaching conversation. The initial reaction is often a mix of amusement or slight offense, but as the conversation goes on, people struggle to answer this question. "I don't care/I like everything/I don't know" are not good answers, I can tell you that.

Figuring out your "thing" is nothing more than Personal Branding. Define yourself in a maximum of two words. "Independent Hunter," "Reliable Leader," "Online Marketer," or even "CA (Corporate Asshole)" are all clearer and more memorable than vague statements.

Making choices and showing empathy and respect for your conversation partner by taking Shape is Personal Branding.

Think of it like a casual meetup where you run into a stranger. The fact that someone says "hello" doesn't give you the green light for a lengthy monologue. By navigating through different phases of the conversation, both parties can either disengage or delve deeper. Maybe it stays at introductions, mentioning your profession and the company you work for, but perhaps there are enough common points to continue talking.

Great, personal branding. Heard of it, sounds good. How do I start?

Start with what's different.

Growing up in the Netherlands in the 1970s, not only did people give me a hard time because I was taller than everyone, but I also had this ridiculous last name: Kennedy. Every roll call, there came the jokes. The adults had history with JFK and Robert Kennedy, and they had a good laugh when they heard it applied to this tall, gawky kid.

Universal truth: Everyone in the class gets teased about something, sometime.

It wasn't until I entered the workforce that I started to see the benefits. The name was memorable, worked for speakers of multiple languages because it's famous, and it carried a positive association with a time when the USA had...let's say, a more positive brand image.

Decades later, I heard an incredible speaker with another tease-inducing last name, Sally Hogshead, say something I'll never forget:"Different is better than better. Different doesn't try to turn you into something else. Different allows you to highlight the singular traits you already have within you. You aren't necessarily better than your competition. But you are already different...If you want to be even more successful, don't change who you are, become more of who you are."

She talked about why people make the decision to buy or choose something. It's not about being better than the alternatives—because better is temporary (especially in the tech world) and it's subjective—what's great for one person may not be relevant for another.

If you want to compete on the playing field of "better," you'll spend a lot of money and time trying to break through. But when you're different, you've already broken through...you are not for everyone, and that's (more than) OK.

"Different is better than better. Different doesn't try to turn you into something else. Different allows you to highlight the singular traits you already have within you. You aren't necessarily better than your competition. But you are already different... If you want to be even more successful, don't change who you are, become more of who you are."

-Sally Hogshead

TRY THIS: Dial Up Your Different

You can start by grabbing a friend or gathering a small group together. You can tackle these exercises solo, but it's way tougher (like tweezing your eyebrows—painful and nearly impossible to get the right angle).

You can mix it up by doing the exercises yourself, sharing your results, and then helping someone else with theirs.

Go Back in Time:

• Remember Edwin's experience of being bullied in school, as discussed in the previous chapter (or check out many celebrities' bios). Often, what gets you called out in the schoolyard can later become a powerful asset. Did this happen to you? What were you taunted for back then, and how are you using that now?

• Think back to activities you loved before you felt pressured to be "good" at them or only pursue them if they led to a job. What were they?

• What's something that has always come naturally to you?

Party Pitch Karaoke:

• Take turns improvising quick pitches (brief enough to share while waiting in line for a drink at a party) for each other based on randomly selected traits or experiences.

Two Truths and a Brand:

• A twist on "Two Truths and a Lie"—each person presents three potential personal brand statements: two true and one false.

- Partners guess which is false, sparking a conversation about authentic personal branding.

Two-Word Brand:

- Set a timer and brainstorm a list of words that positively describe you and the value you bring.

- Now, combine them to create a two-word brand, like Growth Guide, Creative Collaborator, Adaptable Innovator, Empathetic Leader, Analytical Visionary, or Achievement-Oriented Asshole— you get the idea.

- Once you have a few contenders, take them out for a spin and see which one resonates.

"I am an excitable person who only understands life lyrically, musically, in whom feelings are much stronger than reason. I am so thirsty for the marvelous that only the marvelous has power over me. Anything I can not transform into something marvelous, I let go."

-Anaïs Nin

GET A GRIP ON THE THREE PHASES

Communication is a dance, and timing is the rhythm. Successful deals, sales, and progress hinge on recognizing where you are in three distinct phases: *Too Late, Just in Time, and Too Early.*

Each phase demands a unique approach to engage potential customers effectively.

Too Late: Understanding Missed Opportunities

Imagine trying to sell a coffee maker to someone who just bought one. No matter the discount or features, it's not needed. Recognizing when it's too late to pitch is crucial.

Pushing a product that isn't needed only leads to frustration. Instead, take this opportunity to learn about the customer's future needs and position yourself for their next purchase cycle.

Just in Time: Seizing the Perfect Moment

The sweet spot in sales is the Just in Time phase. Picture this: they had a coffee maker, but it just broke, and they have a big board meeting tomorrow. Score! Your product or service aligns perfectly with the customer's immediate needs. It's rare, but when it happens, it's golden.

The key here is preparation and quick action. By understanding your customer's buying cycle and maintaining consistent communication, you can be ready to strike at the perfect moment.

Too Early: Planting Seeds for Future Sales

When you approach a customer too early, they're not ready to buy. The coffee system they have is working fine. Everything's okay. Here, the focus shifts from selling to branding and relationship-building. Don't underestimate the power of referrals: when someone knows who you are, what you offer, and, most importantly, trusts you, they are more than happy to recommend you.

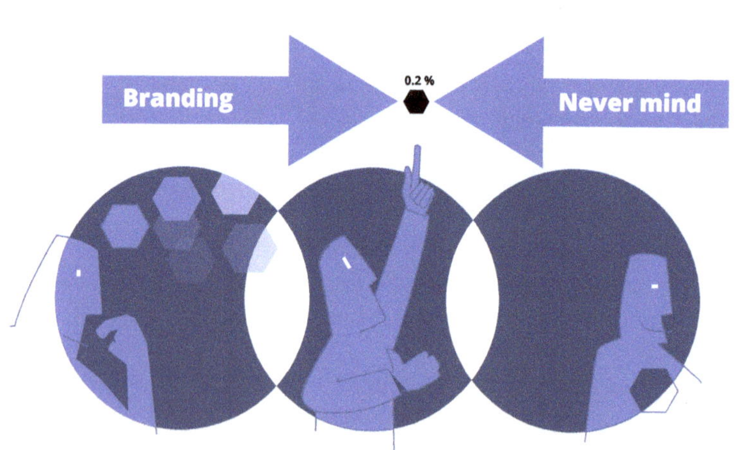

How Do You Get There?

Authenticity is crucial to building trust. Be genuine in your interactions and show respect for your customers' needs and privacy. Understand their buying phases and adjust your approach accordingly. Invest time in developing your personal brand so you can clearly articulate your value.

Share your expertise and provide valuable insights in a three-step process: give, give, give. Establish yourself as a reliable and knowledgeable source. Offer valuable insights and stay top-of-mind so that when the customer is ready, they think of you first.

No amount of pushing is going to make you a deal if it's *Too Early or Too Late*—in fact, it will wreck your chances of ever getting a deal or establishing a useful relationship.

TRY THIS: Think Like Netflix

"The biggest elephant in the marketing room today is that social media is literally free attention. Unlike in decades prior where businesses had to pay hundreds or thousands of dollars for radio, print, billboard and television ads, we now live in a time where it's free to build brand through organic social media posting, and yet most people in the world do not produce nearly enough content for how big the opportunity is."

-Gary Vaynerchuk

To do this, and hopefully position yourself to be the one people think of when they need what you offer, you'll need a steady stream of content.

Just as Netflix offers different genres and types of programming, you will want a mix of educational, inspirational, and product/service focused content (heavier on the first two.)

Over time, this is how people will know and understand your form - what you have to offer the world.

I like to do brainstorming sessions where different people from the organization join me in a room for an hour - with cleared calendars and without their phones.

I ask them to write down (old school with pen and paper) as many responses to these questions as possible while I run a timer.

• What questions do you get asked about this organization/ type of work?

• What have you learned how to do while working here?

• What problems can your team solve?

Since it's all about volume, 'dumb ideas' are welcome.

Pretty sure you will be surprised and start seeing some themes bubble to the top.

Put them all in a list and look at it with a producer's eye: what would make for a good video, a series, a podcast? Have you already made something that answers some of these questions that could be used on different platforms and/or in ongoing communication?

FIND THE FOX

A fox is someone on your side for their own reasons—a person with a special kind of influence. You'll often find them under the radar, quietly pulling strings behind the scenes.

Let me share a story that illustrates just how valuable a fox can be.

I was working for EDS, a big American IT company with its sights set on the entire world of finance. My superiors advised me to close some deals with a few banks, but I saw more possibilities in the insurance sector. Unlike banks, which saw IT as part of their core business and were reluctant to outsource, insurance companies were more open to the idea.

So, I went after it.

My point of contact was Ton from Finance. He told me I had little to no chance of getting EDS in the door and that I might not even get as far as a meeting with Ben, the boss. But thanks to Ton, the meeting happened. There we were: Ben, his management team, my colleague, and myself.

The first thing Ben said when I walked in was, "EDS sucks. They are the worst. If we work with you, it will be over my dead body."

OK.

That's a fun opportunity if you ask me.

"Excellent," I replied. "But what will I get from you if we DO sign a deal?" His answer: "Then I'll connect you with one of my best contacts who has an amazing network and can bring you a ton of business. Guaranteed. But that's an easy promise for me to make because we are never, ever going to work together."

A fascinating start to a meeting. Despite his opening lines, Ben came around a bit, and it turned out to be a pleasant conversation. After we were done, I asked Ton why EDS might not get the deal. He told me, "Ben knows your competitor well—they've been coming here for years and have done good work. At EDS, he only knows you and your colleagues. We have no idea what to expect from you or your company. It seems pretty unlikely that he'd give this plum project to a couple of total strangers."

Despite all that, we made it to the final round. After the last presentation, the insurance company would choose either us or our competitor—the ones they knew well. In high-stakes sales meetings like this, there are usually unwritten rules. One is that you bring as few people as possible, and you have to make a clear case for why each person is in the room. Those rules are excellent, but we decided to go in another direction. Instead of our usual duo, we showed up with nine people, which was a big surprise for everyone.

My chats with Ton, the fox, had made it clear that they would hesitate to go with a total unknown because they didn't know who we were and what we were capable of. By bringing the person in charge of every division delivering this IT project, I got the chance to introduce each of them and explain what they, with their years of hard-won experience, would do for the company and why. I tempered this approach with some humor, poking fun at ourselves a bit, and I saw Ben start to thaw.

We signed the deal, leading to a fantastic collaboration and a successful result. Fortunately, Ben was true to his word and introduced us to
his contact—an even bigger player in the financial sector.

Win-win!

So, What Can You Learn?

- **Don't Disqualify Yourself Early:** Even if you seem down by many points, don't count yourself out at the beginning.

- **Find the Fox:** Identify the influential person behind the scenes and look for ways to shake up the conversation by doing things differently.

- **Influence and Enthusiasm:** Find creative ways to generate enthusiasm and influence the decision-makers.

- **Identify the Real Decision-Maker:** Know who's really responsible for making the purchase decision, or whatever your goal is.

- **Listen, Listen, Listen:** Pay close attention to what's being said (and not said).

- **Speak Their Language:** When you do talk, use the words and phrases that resonate with the fox, hitting the "hot buttons" they've shown you.

Engaging with the fox requires subtlety and tact. It's not about manipulation but about understanding their importance and valuing their input.

By fostering genuine relationships, you can gain valuable insights and support that can be pivotal in closing deals—even, and especially, when you know that your prospect really hates your company.

TRY THIS: Be My Guest

The Secret Weapon for Conquering Any Room

Your heart races, palms sweat, as you enter a bustling event. Everyone seems to know each other, engaged in animated conversations. You? You're radiating what an expert naturalist
might call "Deer In Headlights Energy." We've all been there.

But what if a simple mental trick could transform you from wallflower to life of the party—even on Zoom calls?

Years ago, a wise woman noticed my deer-like state at a formal
affair and whispered a game-changing tip in my ear:
"Pretend this is your party, and everyone here is your guest."

It blew my mind.

This simple shift in perspective is pure genius. Why? Because it instantly:

• Redirects your focus outward

• Silences that pesky inner critic

• Empowers you to take control

(**Spoiler alert:** Most people aren't thinking about you at all. They're probably wondering how much longer they have to stay or if they should have worn something else.)

Now, you're no longer a nervous attendee—you're the gracious host. You're Lumière, the singing, scene-stealing, charismatic candlestick in *Beauty and the Beast*.

You have purpose. You have power. You have permission to:

• Warmly inquire about someone's day

• Ask if they found the venue easily

• Recommend the mouthwatering ceviche

• Approach that person hugging the wall and offer a genuine compliment

• Play matchmaker, connecting people with shared interests

• Ensure everyone's comfortable before you start your presentation

So, the next time you feel that familiar panic rising, remember: This is your party. These are your guests. They're all here for a good time.

Step into every room as the host—welcoming, engaging, and confident—and watch as the energy transforms around you.

"It's so simple, yet makes such a difference. Pretend that every single person you meet has a sign around his or her neck that says, 'Make me feel important.'"

-Mary Kay Ash

Getting psyched up to sell

GROWTH = BOOKKEEPING

I recently listened with a big grin to the legendary football coach Louis van Gaal as he spoke to the Dutch hockey team at the Paris Olympics: "You all know how to play hockey, but trust me: it's all about discipline, team, and focus."

Now, that might sound blunt (and, of course, it is), but anyone who knows Van Gaal will just shrug—he's making the same point I've been hammering home for years in industries like IT.

Having a great product isn't enough to drive growth. If you want to create real value, at some point, you need to generate revenue,
and that doesn't happen by simply hoping customers will flock to you. Sales is a craft, and selling is just like bookkeeping: with discipline, focus, and the right team, you've already got at least a 90% chance of success.

A perfect example of this is the almost obsessive way EDS implemented the Strategic Value Selling method developed by Holden International. Holden created a custom approach for EDS, treating sales as a cycle with four phases: Discover, Define, Confirm, and Deliver.

The key was recognizing that real value lies in investing in existing customers, not in chasing new business, as so many companies mistakenly believe. I often challenge people by saying, "You only need new customers because you want to have more current customers."

After all, nothing eats up more time than building a relationship with a new account from scratch. It can take months of conversations and tough negotiations over the smallest details. In contrast, a solid existing relationship might just call to say the contract is renewed or expanded—a five-minute conversation versus an intense months-long process.

If you're going to put in that kind of effort for a new client, it's essential to qualify them properly—and it's best to do that upfront. According to the SVS method, each phase was critically analyzed before moving forward, but once the numbers were in, there was full commitment for the next period.

This approach was ruthless: one topic focused on competition, and if you didn't know exactly who your competitor was, you started at a -4 (the lowest score), which meant automatic rejection for the next phase. It was immediately clear why we might lose, and as a team, you knew exactly what you needed to find out to proceed. This way, nearly every deal they pursued was won, and the teams operated with a winner's mentality, working efficiently. Everyone in the organization used the same method, so everyone spoke the same language.

So, it's bookkeeping—not some romantic notion of how great things could be or how big someone's ego is. Respect your colleagues, understand the importance of everyone's role, respect other people's time management, show up on time, and come prepared.

It's rarely, if ever, just about the technology, price, knowledge, or anything like that.

As Van Gaal says: Team, Focus, Discipline. Only then does growth happen.

MSCH
TTES

MAXIMIZE YOUR WINS: THE FORMULA FOR SALES SUCCESS

If sales are like bookkeeping—a matter of structured, sometimes tedious work—how can you use this fact to increase your chances of winning?

Winning is rarely just luck.

From my experience, three key elements can significantly boost your chances of success:

1. A sharp qualification using the 4 Magical Questions from the Kennedy Method

2. A rock-solid Value Proposition

3. A Competitive Strategy

The 4 Magic Questions

Whenever an opportunity arises for the teams I work with, I ask four crucial qualifying questions: Do we want this customer? Do we want this deal? Can we deliver? And how can we win?

1. **Do we want this customer?** Or, more precisely, how badly do we want this customer? This question gauges the strategic importance of securing a contract with a potential client. We're not just after a one-off deal but an active reference who can open doors to their network.

2. **Do we want this deal?** What does this contract mean for us in terms of revenue and potential growth? This helps us determine if the deal aligns with our long-term goals.

3. **Can we deliver?** This is where we ensure buy-in from our delivery team, preventing the sales team from tossing a deal "over the wall" to the rest of the organization. It's crucial to secure the operations team's commitment to allocate the necessary resources.

Only if the answers to questions 1-3 are a clear yes do we move on to the fourth question:

4. **How can we win?** Here, we assess our Value Proposition, our network and connections, and the competition. This is where strategy meets execution.

You can always be qualifying in one sense or another, constantly refining your approach.

Value Proposition

A strong Value Proposition can make all the difference. Originating from the Holden Company's Strategic Value Selling approach, a Value Proposition articulates what customers get when they choose your product or service. For example, at SalesPulse, we might say:

"For entrepreneurs looking to boost their sales by at least 100% in one year, SalesPulse is the commercial partner. We do this by leveraging our knowledge and network, spanning two generations—from digital marketing to top-notch executive sales power—at a fraction of the cost of a traditional team."

A Value Proposition isn't just a catchy slogan; it's a clear statement of what customers can expect from your company. Even in markets flooded with competitors offering similar products, each company can have a unique Value Proposition. That's why at SalesPulse, we invest time in the foundation of our sales process; after crafting a compelling Vision, we translate it into a Value Proposition that sets our partners apart from the rest.

Competitive Strategy

Consider the strategy used by EDS, a company that fully embraced this mindset. They believed that a customer doesn't necessarily choose the best product but rather the best alternative. Imagine (and forgive the crass analogy): you're searching for a partner, ideally with blonde hair because you like blondes. But if you're stranded on an island with only redheads, your criteria quickly adjust—and you start looking for the most suitable partner within this new context.

EDS applied this principle to focus intently on outmaneuvering the competition. Their goal was not just to have the best proposal but to ensure they stood out compared to others.

Winning isn't guaranteed, but it's certainly not random, either.

As Bobby Knight famously said, "The key is not the will to win... everybody has that. It is the will to prepare to win that is important."

SIDE NOTE: 20 (Good) Questions

To get your wheels turning, here's a sampler platter of some of our favorite questions.

1. What drew you to this company/field/type of work?

2. What will your company look like in three years?

3. What about in three months? End of this year?

4. What does your ideal day look like?

5. What do you wish people knew about your country/company/industry/daily challenges?

6. Can you walk me through your current process/tech stack/marketing mix?

7. What's the challenge that keeps you up at 3 a.m.?

8. What has your experience been like trying to solve this problem?

9. In an ideal world, how would you solve this problem, regardless
of budget or resources?

10. What obstacles could get in the way of making this happen?

11. What would happen in this situation if you didn't do anything?

12. What's something you're doing now that you wish you could delegate or automate?

13. How do you measure success?

14. How would you describe the perfect partnership with a consultant/vendor? How has that gone for you in the past?

15. How are you evaluated by your boss/board/team?

16. Who else is involved in the decision-making process?

17. What is the best food someone should try when they visit?

18. What sets you/your organization/your country apart?

19. Is there anything you hoped to learn or cover that we haven't touched on yet?

20. What would people be surprised to know about you/your organization?

Always tie back to their goals, dreams, and vision.

As Edwin puts it: "Ask everything and assume nothing. Ever."

TRUST YOUR GUT: 30-SECOND DECISION-MAKING

Much to the horror of anyone who's studied decision-making, I make most of my decisions within 30 seconds.

The Kennedy Theory behind this is simple: "Even if you think long and hard about something, there's still a chance it might go wrong. If you decide quickly, that percentage is about the same. So why not decide right away?" It might sound simplistic, but the math holds up.

When hiring new colleagues, I often decide within 30 seconds. During the hour-long interview, I use open questions to see if my first impression holds up. Almost always, it does. When I second-guess myself, I regret it later.

I've learned that a person's energy, character, and the connection we establish are the foundation of a good working relationship. Nothing is more important than a good rapport with the team. When the spirit is there, knowledge follows. I aim to establish initial contact quickly. If it feels right, the dialogue flows naturally, and you understand each other better.

In a job application process, both parties check each other to see if they want to work together. Candidates, especially, pay close attention to how they're treated. Yet, how often do organizations try to make the hiring process one-sided? They throw dozens of questions at candidates, most of which are redundant because the answers are already on the resume or LinkedIn profile.

The conversation goes much smoother when you ask friendly, open questions that matter to the candidate: "What do you love to do the most? What does your ideal job look like? What kind of employer attracts you and why? What are your ambitions? Why are you interested in our company/this job? Considering your passions, hobbies, and home life, what's your good work rhythm?"

On the flip side, candidates often walk in with shaky knees, just hoping to get the job. It's natural to be nervous, but have you found all the information you were looking for? Is this the employer and job you're excited about, or are you just saying yes to everything?

Looking for a new job brings mixed emotions. On one hand, there's the excitement of seeking something new, an adventure. On the other hand, there's the fatigue that comes with the search.

I firmly believe in the power of recruiting and headhunting, but your network is even more powerful in practice. Remember, recruiters can't perform miracles, and timing is crucial for them, too. Get to know them before you're actively searching so they can keep you in mind.

Job hunting is like having a job; you must constantly network. Even when it's unnecessary, I make sure to have at least one meeting each week just because it's nice to talk to someone. Often, it's about giving and sharing, and it usually stops there. That feeling is pleasant for me, and maybe, just maybe, I can ask for a favor someday. But if not, that's okay too.

Long ago, I was offered a fantastic job at a company with roots in the UK and India. The task was simple: We were very successful in those countries and wanted to reach the same level in Continental Europe (CE). My challenge, my BHAG (Big Hairy Audacious Goal), was the perfect one-liner. Small problem: After two months, I was told that the focus had changed to only India and the UK. They asked if I could shut down CE, lay off everyone, and transfer the clients to other regions.

That evening, after receiving the news from the CEO, I sat with my colleague Richard to discuss how to handle this. Literally, on a beer coaster, an idea was born: The closure would cost a certain amount, but if we could share half of this amount with a new owner, they would get a great group of clients and employees, and we would save the current owner half of the planned costs. Richard called it "A Cunning Plan, Edwin!"

From that moment, the search for a new owner began. The Kennedy Theory could be applied directly. A few days earlier, I had spoken with the two owners of a fast-growing group of IT companies keen on investing in acquisitions. We called them at 10 PM, explained the plan, and met the next morning for breakfast. A few days later, the deal was sealed, demonstrating the power of networking.

Top Takeaways:

Trust Your Gut: Quick decisions often hold up as well as those you agonize over. When your instincts tell you something within the first few moments, pay attention.

Prioritize Connection in Hiring: A good working relationship is built on energy, character, and connection. When the rapport is strong, skills and knowledge naturally follow.

Mutual Respect in Interviews: The hiring process should be a two-way street. Ask meaningful, open-ended questions that allow the candidate to share their story, and show that you're genuinely interested in what they bring to the table.

The Power of Networking: Networking isn't just about finding a job; it's about maintaining relationships that could lead to unexpected opportunities. Make networking a regular part of your routine, even when you're not actively searching.

Flexibility in Business: Be ready to pivot when circumstances change. Sometimes, a quick, creative solution can turn a setback into an opportunity—like finding a new owner to keep a business running.

PRACTICE YOUR CHESS MOVES: SCENARIO THINKING

Sometimes, I notice that I am entirely losing people during a conversation.

I might be reasoning thoughtfully, discussing a possible approach or the chances of winning a deal, thinking I'm being constructive.

But then I catch a look from the other side of the table that says, "Thanks for raining on my parade. Didn't expect you to be such a downer."

After some reflection, I realized this only happens when I'm thinking in a natural way that can be confusing for others:

Scenario Thinking.

It's a fact: good chess players are almost always scenario thinkers. Scenario thinkers are often chess players. Chess players try to anticipate which moves might lead to which responses.

Sometimes, this involves dozens of moves with hundreds of possible countermoves. You never know exactly how your opponent will react, but you can get pretty far by mapping out potential scenarios. Every move results in a response, and every reaction changes the playing field again.

There's little as enjoyable as training the brain this way, but some people only get headaches from it. They prefer just to make a move or propose something to step out of the metaphor. It saves a lot of overthinking, but the chance of underestimating the opponent is significantly higher.

Scenario Thinking is a powerful tool that allows us to examine complex problems or challenges from various angles, almost like stepping into the future. While we can't literally do that, by exploring and discussing different possibilities, we can gain a sense of what that future might look like.

What actions will likely lead to what outcomes?

By thinking beyond our own perspective, we can consider how others—competitors, prospects, or customers—might see things. This approach enlightens us and empowers us to make more informed decisions.

When putting together a proposal, I like to jot down the key features and think about how different people (from the customer's side) might react. We naturally tend to focus on our view: what's good about our proposal, what our USPs (Unique Selling Points) are, how hard our team is working, and how smart we are. That's all very normal and human.

But your perspective sharpens when you think like the "devil's advocate":

What's wrong with the proposal?

Where are the weak spots?

What can be improved?

Have we really done everything we can?

Playing this role and discussing it openly brings new insights.

If you dare to incorporate these, your proposal/job interview/ project can reach the next level.

TRY THIS: Embrace Scenario Thinking (and Ace Your Next Job Interview)

I admit that I'm the person who resists envisioning worst-case scenarios and tends to check out when Edwin pushes me to do so.

But when I approached it with a lighter mindset, I found myself willing to try it—and started to see just how useful it could be in all kinds of situations.

Here are a few ways to start playing this kind of chess:

1. **Daily Decision Exercise:** For a week, write down one decision you made each day and imagine three different outcomes. How does it feel to flex those mental muscles?

2. **Future Playlist:** Create a playlist that represents different potential futures. How does each song reflect a possible outcome?

3. **Alternative Endings:** Choose a familiar movie and brainstorm alternative endings. How would these changes affect the entire story? This exercise demonstrates how small changes can lead to vastly different outcomes.

4. **Random Word Exercise:** Open a book to a random page, choose a word, and relate it to your current project or problem. How might this unexpected element change future scenarios?

5. **Personal SWOT Analysis:** For the corporate readers, conduct a personal SWOT analysis (Strengths, Weaknesses, Opportunities, Threats) for different scenarios.

6. **Life in Ten Years:** Write a detailed description of a day in your life ten years from now. Create three versions based on different current decisions.

7. **Reverse Engineering:** Start with a desired future outcome. You can work backward, listing the steps and decisions that might lead to that result.

If you're working with a partner or a small group, try these exercises:

1. **What If Chain:** Take turns asking "What if" questions about a simple situation (e.g., "What if it rains on our parade?"). Each person adds a new "What if" to build a chain of scenarios.

2. **Scenario Ping-Pong:** Play a mental ping-pong, alternating between sharing best-case and worst-case scenarios.

Job Interview Preparation:

Scenario thinking can revolutionize how you prepare for a job interview.

Edwin encouraged me to push myself to think of the most challenging, worst interview questions that could come up—the ones that poke directly at a weakness I'd rather conceal. Then, come up with a way to answer them.

If these questions surface (I've found they often don't - and I am sometimes a bit disappointed by that because I was READY), you won't be caught off guard.

Better yet, you've faced some of your fears and done something about them, which can only boost your confidence. Plus, being super-prepared frees up your mind to listen better to what your interviewer is—and isn't—saying.

CONSIDER CULTURAL DIFFERENCES

Take a business trip, and you'll spot them: the tall, blond Dutchman, booming in the hotel lobby, barking orders at the staff. The Dutch seem to cling to the belief that "If I shout loudly enough, everyone will understand me—no interpreter needed."

Once upon a time, traders from our tiny nation roamed the world, conquering territories and sealing lucrative deals. Mistakes? Never. We even traded what would become New York for a sugar colony in the Caribbean...

Honestly, I still see the descendants of those traders conducting business the same way. Especially in banking—they love sending the "Great White Man" to foreign lands to explain how the world works. It's painfully embarrassing.

But it's not just the Dutch. India, for instance, has a similar strategy for any IT challenge: send another team to Europe or the USA, and all will be well. Chinese IT firms are catching on too, holding weekend meetings so their Western colleagues can't participate, and by Monday, the cards are already dealt.

And the United States? Don't get me wrong—I'm a fan of America. It's a beautiful country with stunning landscapes, and we owe a lot to our American allies. But Americans often lack a trait that Europeans cherish: self-mockery. Watching Americans tell Italians how to make and drink coffee makes my toes curl. And I cringe when an American orders a dish only to customize it into oblivion—spaghetti Bolognese without tomatoes, without cheese, without meat... you get the idea.

That said, working with Americans is a blast. They're driven, motivated, and fiercely competitive. They hit the gym early and work long hours to push their Team to new heights. The contrast is stark when you consider the French businessman's joke: he couldn't understand why his company struggled—after all, he'd worked a whole 12 hours that week...

Many of our SalesPulse clients are highly successful international enterprises looking to expand in Europe. I always advise them to work as much as possible with locals. Europe is a patchwork of cultures: the Nordics with their advanced social systems, Germany's many faces from Berlin to Munich, and France, where your business school alma mater dictates your relationships.

Then you have the Catalans, the Basques, Northern and Southern Italy, Corsica, and so on. And let's not even get started on England, Scotland, Ireland, etc. Here's the easiest myth to debunk: "Benelux" doesn't exist, folks. There's a massive cultural gap between the tiny Netherlands, Belgium, and Luxembourg. Tossing these three (or four, considering Flemish and Walloons) under one manager is a recipe for disaster.

So, I decided to do things differently. I took a course to polish my English and understand American culture better.

Even more importantly, I wanted to grasp the differences between colleagues and clients from Texas, Atlanta, and New York—where our offices were and where I worked with various teams. My teacher, Kate, tried to hammer home that the world didn't revolve around me (breaking news!) and that listening is an art.

I joke about it, but it's a real struggle to show respect, understand, listen, and adapt to other countries and cultures. If you can stay true to yourself while adapting, you've got a shot at making it as an international businessperson.

My reward came ten years later in India when some colleagues called me "adaptable." I'll admit, I was proud. But more importantly, I understood just how crucial adaptability is if you want to succeed beyond your borders.

SIDE NOTE: "Are Your Parents in the Circus?"

or, How the Dutch helped me grow (not literally)

Did he really just say that?

I was in the middle of a roaring frat party, and a giant guy (over six feet like all of his friends) was patting me on the top of my head and saying, "Your parents, back in America— are they in the circus? Ha ha ha!"

Welcome to the Netherlands, home of radical candor and cheerful equal-opportunity offenders. ("If we didn't like you, we wouldn't make fun of you so much!")

Making like Dutch Masters in Amsterdam with my friend (and former department store colleague) Sabine.

If you've ever found it tiring trying to figure out what people really mean, you will love it. Here, the truth is considered a gift that is freely given - along with a saying for literally every possible situation.

Here are three that illustrate some of the great lessons I learned (and still draw upon today, especially when it's time to change the ground rules.)

1. "No, you already have - yes, you can get!"

(Nee heje, ja kenje krijge) This phrase encourages asking for what you want. As a Southern American might say, "Ain't nobody never got nothin' that they didn't ask for." Or, in the words of Dutch soccer legend Johan Cruijff: "If you don't shoot, you always miss."

2. "Just glue 'em behind the wallpaper."

From a 1930s novel, here's what you can do (figuratively) with the people who are annoying you and taking up too much space in your head.

3. "Every morning, the King and I sit on the same throne."

It is tough to be intimidated when considering this earthy visual, which incorporates another non-taboo subject for the Dutch: gastrointestinal functions. (PS When working in a fancy department store, my colleagues thought it would be funny to have me, "Our kind of legal worker from New York," go help her. Reader, she was very kind. We chose a scarf, and she went on to shoes. Not sure if she stopped at the restroom.)

WORK FOR A WIN-WIN

(AND CHECK OUT INDIA)

India is one of the most beautiful countries I know, and rarely have I felt as much warmth as with the Indians: Smart, friendly, well-educated, and incredibly hospitable. When I once had the unique opportunity to represent an Indian company as a pioneer, I was eager with anticipation.

My task was to establish a presence for a major Indian player in Continental Europe. My starting point: 3 Indians scattered across Belgium, Germany, and the Netherlands

One of my first memories came during the application process: could I be in New Delhi in two days to spend Saturday with the two most important executives? I took a red-eye flight, landing in the early morning, brushed my teeth, and then spent the whole day in conversation with Mr. Raman and Sujit in a beautiful new hotel in the old city. The hotel hadn't officially opened yet, so it was an excellent opportunity to see what I thought of it (the first but certainly not the last time I heard an Indian say the famous "Win-Win").

The conversation went as it ideally should but rarely does in the West: I spent the entire day talking formally and informally with both gentlemen, getting to know and understand each other. By the end of the day, I was highly motivated to take on this challenge.

Around 3 in the afternoon, our hosts realized we hadn't had lunch yet. No problem; what did I feel like eating? Strangely enough, they suggested Japanese cuisine, and we went in that direction. Just as we arrived, I noticed the lights go out, and the restaurant closed after lunch. My host, Sujit, indicated that we still wanted to have lunch. Without any issue, doors flew open, lights came on, and we were warmly welcomed again—a slightly different mentality than in the average Western establishment.

The service was impressive during our conversations, and my host asked for my opinion. I, the clumsy Dutchman, naturally had some tips... I, for instance, felt slightly uncomfortable with the ladies who watched every table with no other purpose than turning the ashtrays.

He asked me if I had an idea of these ladies' salaries. I mentioned a figure, and he informed me that it was only 10% of that amount. Then he asked me what she could do with that amount. I suspected she needed at least two extra jobs to meet ends. Sujit explained that with this amount, she could support her entire family (!).

These ladies had well-paying jobs, their families could live excellently on them, the hotel had highly motivated staff for a decent amount, and the customer was catered to every whim. You guessed it: Win-Win...

In the following weeks, I also experienced the flip side of business in India. As we all thought, the conversation had gone exceptionally well, and an offer was supposed to come within a few days. A month later, there was still no word, and I couldn't continue reminding them without losing face.

In consultation with my contact there, I decided to take a different approach. A rumor was circulating that the CEO would be at Schiphol that afternoon for team discussions (you could never be sure…). I knocked, walked in, and received a warm welcome from CEO Mr. Raman. He was curious about how my start had been. When I explained that I still didn't have a contract, he shrugged (we know each other, Edwin, right?) and shouted to the team that the contract had to be done now. There was no need to read, just sign a warm handshake, and I was on board.

Indeed, the introduction in Europe involved a few days of conversation with the three individuals there, so I was initially placed in India, first in Delhi, then in Chennai, and briefly in Bangalore. Upon arriving in Delhi, I immediately received an invitation from HR manager Shantanu. He suggested that I move into a residence belonging to an executive stationed in the US for a few years. The house had all the facilities, with a staff of 12 (!), and I incurred fewer expenses by staying there. The US colleague's residence was safe (another Win-Win…). Upon arrival, I was warmly welcomed into Shantanu's home the same evening, where he lived with his young family (pregnant wife and son).

I value my privacy a lot, but I have never felt so quickly and genuinely welcomed. The family felt like a warm embrace, and to this day, we stay in touch, making them feel like family on the other side of the world.

Living in a house instead of a hotel and being a daily guest at their home quickly gave me more insight into the real India: I could ask anything, get answers to everything, and go anywhere with them. I went to the local market with Shantanu's lovely wife and witnessed the most refined woman in India negotiate fiercely over a figurine I wanted to buy. My suggested price of 100 Euros was scoffed at, and

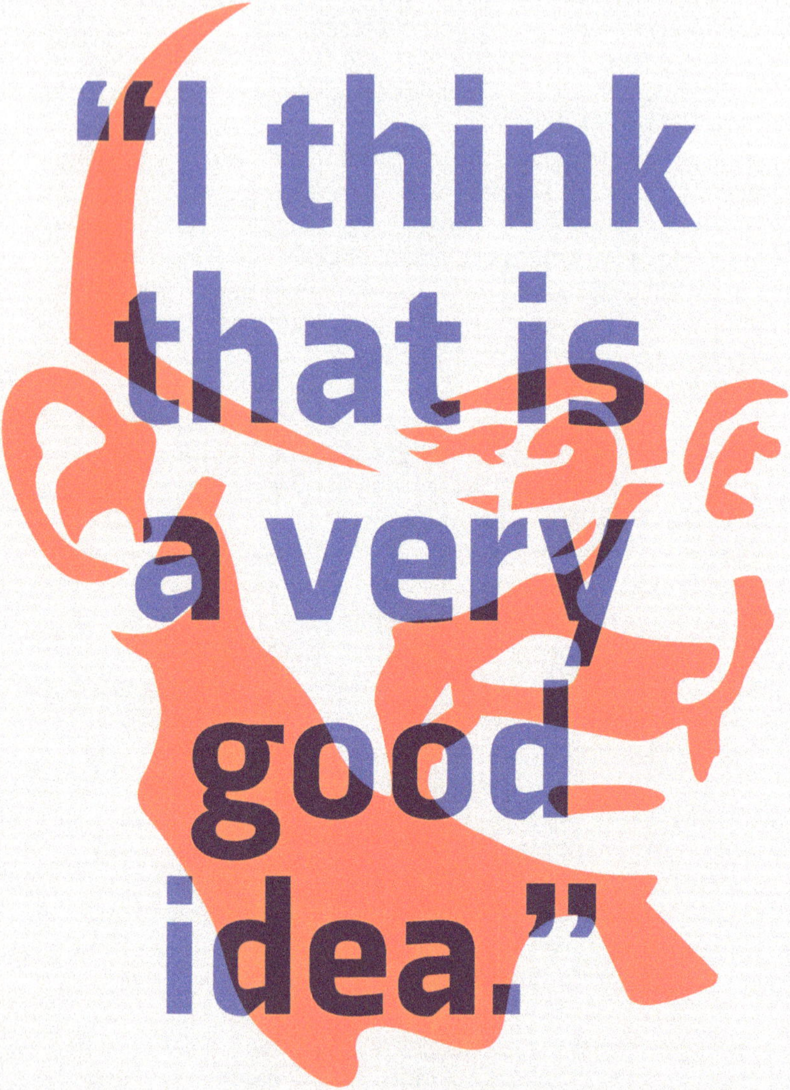

"I think that is a very good idea."

eventually, the Ganesha figurine was in my possession for 3 Euros and 50 cents.

The salesperson had been insulted in every possible way, accused of terrible things, and almost crawled behind us to apologize. And yet they were still satisfied!

I spent the rest of the day in complete bewilderment watching her. No corporate negotiation training could compare to this experience.

A remarkable moment was the conversation with the family about my disabled son, Aaron. According to Shantanu and his wife, this was unfortunate for us, but it could be easily resolved with a visit to their temple.

On a beautiful Sunday, we went there and were warmly welcomed by the community leader. He listened to the issue, nodded understanding, and walked me to one of the temples. There, I shared a photo of Aaron, offered a piece of fruit, and witnessed an impressive scene with the attending priest. Finally, I received a piece of nougat wrapped in aluminum foil with the request to store it in the freezer and bring it home. Please give it to my son, and everything will be fine.

When I flew back to the Netherlands a few weeks later, Shantanu ensured the piece went with me in my carry-on. I had completely forgotten about it until I raised eyebrows at security, which led to me being taken aside into a room. It took an hour of talking, explaining, calling, and pleading until everyone understood the story, and I (a bit startled) was allowed to take my seat on the plane.

Unsurprisingly, the effectiveness at home was a bit disappointing, but I still smile when I think about the love and care I felt from the genuine intentions of these kind people.

India's got some not-so-great sides, too, like the infamous Delhi Belly – a nasty stomachache where everything makes a swift exit ("easy come, easy go"). A quick tip: if you're flying back from India, steer clear of the seats near the toilet. I had my moment, and luckily, it happened while I was still at the house, just two seconds away from the bathroom dash. The next day, when the news spread that I was sick, there was a bit of a fuss – not the kind of hosting they liked. Looking concerned, Mr. Raman called me in and assured me they had a doctor in the office building ("one of the best, Edwin, one of the best.")

Resisting didn't work, and five minutes later, I found myself in the office of this miracle worker. The walls were all glass, and to my horror, the entire room was filled with a thick smoke haze. Once inside, I met a friendly guy who proudly shared that he watched all football matches in the Netherlands live on TV in India. This guy smoked like a chimney and barely slept at night – not exactly reassuring. After some examination, he had a straightforward explanation for my illness: "In India, you have bacteria that you don't have in the Netherlands, and they were in your food, making you really sick." According to him, it would pass on its own.

However, there was a problem in his eyes: "If I let you go outside now without medicine, I have a credibility issue, so please cooperate." The doctor called in a young man who was instructed to fetch various medicines from the pharmacy. When he returned 10 minutes later, the doctor asked me to walk out with the paper bag prominently visible and take it home. Flush everything down the toilet, go to bed on time, rest, and please provide a positive reference tomorrow (this was pre-Google Reviews.) The next day, it did get a bit better, and I proudly informed Mr. Raman that, indeed, he had one of the best doctors ever on staff. Mr. Raman is happy, and doctor is happy; I'm so glad; you know the drill by now: Win-Win.

I started to get the hang of how this whole hierarchy thing worked, and sometimes, I even liked it. The smart and driven CEO was also among the founders, so everyone automatically respected him. It hit me during my first trip to India. In the beginning, Mr. Raman asked me to drop by after a few weeks to give him an update. So, on a nice day, I strolled to his office. But, peeping through the glass walls, I saw him deep in discussion with a group. I flashed a friendly smile through the glass, turned around, and returned to my desk. Surprisingly, his door swung open within seconds, and he hollered that he'd come to me in a bit. I thanked him and headed back to my colleagues. They were waiting, looking at me like, "Mr. Raman stepped out for you, you know what that means, right?"

In that same hierarchy, I got a lesson when Sujit visited our office in the Netherlands. After the warmest greetings (never forget the first 10 minutes with someone from India, discussing the journey, family, health, etc.), he was eager to know if his team in Chennai was assisting me well with the proposal. I enthusiastically shared about their dedication and quality, which pleased him. His next question was about whether everything was on schedule.

When I mentioned we had a slight delay, my esteemed colleague exploded. Within 2 minutes, he had a team of 20 people on a call, passionately expressing his disappointment: he was ashamed and thoroughly annoyed, and this went on for 15 minutes in a manner that would raise eyebrows elsewhere. Then he hung up and chatted casually with me.

Surprisingly, no one was upset; they appreciated the clarity. I'd have a big problem in the Netherlands if I spoke like that, but here, it was fine, and everyone moved on. It's tough but very clear. The proposal got even better, was delivered on time, and we secured the client.

Back in the Netherlands, we slowly began positioning the company, and a former client of mine expressed interest in chatting. They remembered me, and the timing seemed right as they explored options. Based on past experiences, I made it to the long list, allowing us to pitch to the board. As other Indian companies dropped out after several sessions, we became the preferred supplier for this major international insurer.

We clinched this deal because we were the only ones augmenting the team with Dutch expertise.

While competitors sent (increasingly) Indians to the prospect, I could consistently be the thread in our team. This allowed us to listen well instead of just presenting, and I understood the customer's needs: they wanted to start with a few small projects to ease in and learn, avoiding a direct Big Bang approach.

This way, we could discuss the differences in approach and explore how to enhance classical communication models. We started with three deals of up to 100,000 Euros each but worked with over 600 employees for this client for over ten years.

I actually feel at home in many countries. But landing in Delhi, walking out of the airport, seeing the colors, hearing the hustle and bustle, and taking in the unique smells does something to me.

BRIDGE THE GAP: BUILDING TEAMS THAT SPAN GENERATIONS

In today's fast-paced digital world, staying relevant means constantly learning and adapting. Terms like "Digital Transformation" and "ContinuousNext" aren't just buzzwords—they're reminders that there's always something new on the horizon, and it's coming at you fast.

To ride these waves of change and not get left behind, you've got to embrace what I call the Generation Advantage in your network, company, and mindset. Building teams that span different generations isn't just about diversity for diversity's sake; it's about bringing together a range of perspectives and strengths to solve problems creatively and keep the client front and center.

Take a story from fifteen years ago when I was setting up financial technology for an insurance company. One of the

"A path is created when you walk on it."

- Zhuang Zi

founders, Frank, a seasoned marketer, teamed up with a young colleague he introduced as his CFO—Chief Facebook Officer. And no, that wasn't a joke. This young woman, barely in her 20s, had years of experience with social media and single-handedly tapped into an entirely new target group.

What made their collaboration work was mutual respect. They didn't boss each other around with "This is how we're doing it." Instead, they shared their methods and learned from each other. That's how the insurer managed to connect with two completely different audiences.

A CEO once told me his biggest headache was constantly hunting for young people with fresh experiences who could predict what's coming next. "As soon as they're on board," he said, "I'm already looking for their replacements because I know another opportunity will come along, and things will change."

It sounds exhausting—and it is—but it's also a pretty sharp take on today's challenges. New developments hit like lightning, and it's tough to get and keep the experience needed to manage and capitalize on them.

Look at the successful folks in cloud and hosting companies. They're often between 25 and 35, rarely worked under a boss, and have been entrepreneurs since they were kids. Many are already well-off, yet they dress casually, work when and where they want, and are all about iterating, learning, and delivering results.

I've got a lot of respect for how these entrepreneurs operate, and I learn from them every day.

But sometimes, they remind me of old-school execs who just can't break out of their mental boxes. Like the CIO who once yelled at me, "Our customer data will never be stored online in the cloud because the Central Bank in our country will never allow it!"

These execs often shy away from new ideas and avoid talking directly to the source of innovation. Ironically, they hire firms to guide their digital transformation while they're still trying to catch up themselves.

Forget the usual suspects. Talk to an entrepreneur who's in the trenches, driving the innovation your company needs.

If we focus on helping our customers' customers—bridging generations as we go—we can smash through any ceiling.

How to Get That Generation Advantage:

Build Diverse Teams: Bring in team members from different generations, including Gen Z. This mix gives you a range of perspectives and strengths. With technology and the world changing so quickly, you can't possibly be an expert in every hot trend. Instead, build a team of specialists who excel in their areas and thrive on collaboration and respect. Think of a Formula 1 team: only two drivers get behind the wheel, but they're nothing without a huge team of experts making sure the car is competitive.

Foster Mutual Mentorship: Create a culture where younger and older employees share their knowledge and skills. It's a two-way street that helps everyone grow together.

Recruit Continuously: Always be on the lookout for fresh talent, especially young professionals with new insights and experiences. Don't wait for a vacancy—build your talent pipeline now.

Engage Directly with Innovators: Skip the middleman and connect directly with young entrepreneurs and innovators. They're usually at the forefront of the changes your company needs to stay ahead.

Focus on Clients: Prioritize your clients' needs and those of their customers. Make sure every generation's perspective is considered in your solutions. The more you understand and address these needs, the more likely you are to succeed.

Experience Over Enthusiasm: Younger employees might bring energy and fresh ideas, but they often lack the experience to handle high-pressure situations effectively. Older employees, on the other hand, have weathered plenty of storms and bring a level of calm and resilience that's invaluable. An older mentor once told me, "If you touch me, all my bones will break, but I am much better than you." That's experience talking.

Seasoned pros develop a sharp sense of emotional intelligence. They can quickly tell if someone's genuine or trying to pull a fast one—skills that save companies time and money. This kind of insight comes from years of varied experiences and can't be taught in a workshop.

Set People Loose: And let's not forget: the main job of any real executive, no matter their generation, is to define the target on the horizon—where the organization should be in a few years— and then clearly communicate that vision. "This is where we're headed. Now, who's willing, eager, and able to get us there?"

When the team knows the ultimate goal, daily activities become purpose-driven and transformative. It keeps you out of the weeds of micromanagement, too—you can bring the conversation back to the big goal and ask, "Are we on track?"

That's real empowerment.

4 down...
to go...
Closing celebrations are the best

CHANGE THE GROUND RULES

After more than a year of sweating over proposals, we found ourselves in the final showdown for a major outsourcing deal—a seven-year contract that could change the game. It was down to us and one other vendor. The stakes were high, and we were each given two hours to make our case. We were set to go second, and our competitor knew the game: they dragged out their presentation, hoping to leave the client worn out and itching for the clock to strike.

As we sat in the next room, waiting, I felt a gut instinct kicking in. Without hesitation, I knocked on the door five minutes past their allotted time, walked in with a grin, and said the words that would turn the tide: "If they can't even manage to be on time, I shudder to think how much delay a seven-year project will have." The room froze—my team stared in disbelief, the competition fumed, and the client's CEO muttered, "That Kennedy is an asshole, but he's got a point."

We went in next, and that night, the contract was ours. The cherry on top? A job offer from the rival company. I didn't hesitate to turn it down.

Night Shift

During the final price negotiations for another major deal, we were invited to the client's office at the end of the day. The setup was clear: one room for talks, two separate rooms nearby for each team to strategize.

Now, I knew the CEO wasn't fond of late nights in the office, so we had a plan. An hour into negotiations, the CEO threw out a final price—X amount, take it or leave it. The funny thing? X was 5% above our bottom line. We could have signed right then and there, but after months of dealing with their games, we felt like making them sweat a bit.

I sighed dramatically, shot my team a look, then turned to the client with an even darker glare. "We need to coordinate with HQ in the US," I said. "We can tweak the price, but this is pushing it."

Back in our room, I briefed the team. The mission: drag it out. Look troubled, make phone calls, stare at screens like you're calculating the meaning of life. Just hold out as long as possible.

Hours later, the CEO couldn't take it anymore. He called me back, asking what was taking so long and if there was anything he could do to move things along—he just wanted to go home. Five minutes later, we had a new best offer on the table, adding another 10% to their previous bid.

Over the years, I've always fought to give my clients the best price and support them however I can. But here's the truth: as a client, you might hold the power, but if you don't treat people right, you'll end up paying more in the long run.

Top Tips

Recognize When to Pivot: If you sense your client's interest wavering, it's time to change your approach. A simple question like, "Can you help me understand where things stand?" can re-engage them and bring any concerns to light.

Always Be Qualifying: Continuously assess your client's readiness and priorities. Are they ready to make a decision? Do they care more about price or quality? What are their long-term goals? Knowing these factors helps you tailor your approach.

Address Avoidance: Watch for signs of avoidance. If a client tries to delay with, "Let me send you an agreement," dig deeper. Ask, "What information do you need to decide today?" This helps uncover hidden objections and shows you're proactive.

Turn Up the Heat: Sometimes, a little assertiveness goes a long way. If you notice a client starting to pull back, don't dance around it—bring it up directly. Try saying, "I've noticed you seem less engaged lately. Is there something we need to talk about?" The goal here isn't to push too hard but to clear the air and make sure everyone's still on the same page.

(Calmly) Handle Rejection: If you're turned down, stay professional and plan a follow-up. "Thank you for your honesty. Would it be okay if I checked back in a few months?" This keeps the relationship open for future opportunities.

Don't Let Up in the Last Stretch: Success isn't just about starting strong—it's about finishing even stronger. The last 20% of any deal is often the toughest, but that's where the real victories happen.

"If they don't give you a seat at the table, bring a folding chair."

-Shirley Chisholm

JUST ASK FOR IT

How do you tell a nerd (yep, that's me) from a real deal closer? (Also me.)

A real deal closer is unapologetically proud of their price and knows when it's time to ask for the deal. The last 10%, the close, is the most difficult part of the sales process - so most of the people will focus on the first 90%.

Let me paint a picture for you: a sharp, knowledgeable representative from an outstanding IT company has been in constant touch with a potential client for months. He's built a solid rapport, his product is flawless, and he's addressed every question and concern the prospect could possibly have. But now, he's hit a wall. The deal is just sitting there, ripe for the taking, and yet, our tech-savvy friend can't seem to close.

The solution is almost maddening in its simplicity: ask for the deal. It's easy to get caught up in endless meetings, reassuring yourself that the client isn't ready yet. But here's the truth: they are. They've been ready. You just need to make the ask.

It might feel like a taboo step, but it's critical if you want to grow. Clients in the service industry rarely fall over themselves to sign contracts; they need a nudge—a confident, well-timed push.

Here's a trick to help you over that last hurdle: get your client into a "yes rhythm." It's an old-school tactic, but it works. Think of the classic car salesman: "You wanted the black SUV, right? Leather seats, correct? The test drive was smooth, yes? The price fits your budget, doesn't it?" You're leading them down a path of agreement, and once they're on it, they're more likely to keep saying yes.

Whether you call it Neuro-Linguistic Programming or just savvy salesmanship, the principle is the same. If you want to grow, you need to sell, and selling means asking for the sale. I've said it before, and I'll say it again: whatever field you're in, develop your commercial skills. They're what keep the lights on.

Don't react to the 'what,' respond to the 'why.'

This takes practice. But here's the kicker: the more you listen, the less you talk, and the more intriguing you become. People want to be heard, and when they feel you're really listening, they're more likely to buy in—literally.

"I've got a killer story that will make them want to buy right now," you might think. But here's the harsh reality: more often than not, your presentation will outshine your content. A great product and a charming conversation aren't enough to drive action. People need to know why they should act now, how it's going to benefit them, and, of course, what it's going to cost.

So, the next time you're standing at the edge of closing a deal, remember: the magic lies in just asking for it.

PS If they're asking you what it costs ...they're buying!

TRY THIS: Cold-Calling

The very name might make your blood run cold - getting on the phone and breaking into the day of strangers who aren't waiting for your call.

Spoiler alert: it's not that bad. It's one of the best ways to get over yourself and sharpen your skills in persuasion, persistence, and plain old chutzpah.

Remember (or imagine from movies or tales from your parents) how much fun prank calling could be? Light-hearted, easy, not attached to a particular outcome—ready to try another approach.

A meaningful way to exercise your listening and persuading muscles at the same time is to do phone banking for a political candidate or organization you believe in.

This is often organized so you have support in the form of training, a user-friendly platform, and the presence of other people if you get together to do it in person. I've done this since I was a teenager and have recently found that applying the principles from this book have helped a lot: first, listen to see how the other person is showing up.

Ask good questions. Find common ground. Talk to them like a neighbor. "So, what's important to you in this election? What do you hope to see ? Have you made a plan to vote?" Then ask for what you want. "Will you join us and vote/talk to three of your friends/register/come to the next phone bank?"

You can take those skills to work as well. When I started a job selling a digital marketing platform to nonprofits, Edwin pushed me to apply this same spirit. I had my own list of leads gathered from conferences and research.

Here's how a typical call could go:

"Hello, Foundation for Arctic Exploration; this is Mike. How can I direct your call?"

"Good morning, Mike, it's Kate. How have you been?"

"Uh, good, I guess…" (Mike's trying to remember if he knows me, giving me a read on his mood.)

"Great! Super quick—I'm trying to reach Bob Sled, the Marketing Director. Could you help point me in the right direction?"

"What did you say you were calling about?" (He just gave me the perfect opening for my pitch!)

"Of course! I'm working with foundations like yours around the country to explore ways to raise more money this end-of-year giving season…"

"Well, uh, Bob's pretty tied up with planning meetings. Can I put you through to his voicemail?" (Which is probably full.)

"To make it easy, is someone from his team in the office this morning?"

"Um…Donna might be available…"

"Excellent! What's her extension? I'll try her in a few minutes—really appreciate it."

(I'm going to hang up and call Donna. When she picks up, I'll tell her that Mike suggested I contact her.)

After you've done this enough times, it takes the edge off. You'll get people who say no, who may become annoyed, or who may hang up. And after that happens, you'll realize you're still fine, alive, and there's a whole bunch of other numbers to call. Give it a try for no more than an hour to start with and see how it builds up your confidence!

MAKE WORK WORK FOR YOU

I've been lucky—fortunate enough to craft my own course in life and work. It might sound counter intuitive, but let me be blunt: I really enjoy working!

No joke. Seriously.

For years, the idea of being trapped in an office from 9 to 5, slogging through traffic to get there and back, felt like pure misery. Thankfully, early in my career, I found myself working with teams spread across different continents. By the time I rolled out of bed, teams in India and Australia were already deep into their day. By dinner, my colleagues in North and South America were just getting started.

This setup forced me to rethink the traditional workday—because, let's face it, no one wants to be glued to their desk from 5 AM to 11 PM.

So, I crafted my own rhythm. I took on long days but made sure to break them up with things that actually mattered. Early mornings, I'd dive into emails and get the ball rolling. Then it was off to take the kids to school and hit the gym. I'd head into the office after rush hour and escape before traffic snarled up again.

The goal? Meet with colleagues and clients and steer clear of tasks I could tackle from home or on the go. Late afternoons were family time, then back to work. Weekends? No problem. This approach let me rack up those 105-hour workweeks I mentioned. Sounds crazy, but I loved it—juggling the important stuff while being fully available for clients and colleagues. It gave me more quality time than most people stuck in the typical 32-hour grind.

As time went on, my outlook shifted even more. I almost abandoned the idea of climbing the ladder within just one company. When I started working for an Indian firm, they couldn't quite grasp the Dutch perks—company cars, pensions, insurances—it all seemed like a bureaucratic nightmare to them. So, they suggested a management fee. I'd get a monthly fee through my own company, from which I could manage my salary, car, pension, phone, etc. It was a win-win for everyone (you can check out my earlier piece on the Win-Win in India).

I also grew to love the idea of helping others and getting rewarded for it. My days became a mix of different gigs and roles. After the heartbreaking loss of our youngest son Aaron, the need to earn for his future was sadly gone, and I found a new rhythm. I look for projects where I can commit 2-3 days a week for at least a year. On top of that, I help entrepreneurs unlock their growth potential, and in return, I ask for equity. If equity's not an option, I get a fee, or sometimes a mix of both. I love helping out, but I've learned the hard way to make sure I get my fair share of the pie.

And there's still time to give back—sharing my time, network, and knowledge through platforms like NLGroeit and the Papageno Foundation by Aaltje and Jaap van Zweden.

This way, every day is different. I'm in the thick of things, constantly learning from other companies and people. Work is fun. Really!

SIDE NOTE: Take out the Trash

"No part of your experience is wasted. Everything you've experienced so far is part of what you were meant to learn."
—Martha Beck

I couldn't wait to start working. Even as a young teenager, I wanted to be in the real world, where the action was, and I definitely wanted my own cash to blow on what I considered absolute necessities at the time—bubble skirts, concert tickets, and multiple perms.

One morning, while we were sitting on the porch drinking coffee before I caught the school bus, my father gave me a golden tip: "When you start working," he said, "look for the job nobody else wants. The crummy job. That thing that never gets done and annoys your boss the most? Step up and do it."

I stared at him, puzzled. "Why?"

"Because," he explained, "when you step up to take on what nobody else wants to do, you become the person who Gets Stuff Done. Most likely, others have either failed at it or just ignored it, so even if you don't 'succeed,' you're still making a mark and delivering a benefit. Your boss will notice...and you probably won't have a lot of competition to get the assignment."

Right at that moment, as if on cue, a sanitation truck drove by, and the driver gave him a happy wave, which my dad cheerfully returned. "I don't care if you go drive a garbage truck," he said. "You be the best driver the town has ever seen. Think about how you can do it better and help more people. Make yourself indispensable."

My dad knew what he was talking about. A first-generation college student who left his tiny town with a cardboard suitcase and a scholarship to become a beloved professor, he had firsthand experience. And even when he had 'made it,' he would take on extra work—wallpapering, painting houses, bookkeeping, and more—to help finance the best possible education for me and my sister. He truly believed that every job was worthy and worth doing well.

Edwin and I started working together because I was the teacher of last resort—my boss said he was "difficult," "demanding," and "nobody else wants to work with him." How could I refuse? I'm glad I didn't!

When I left teaching to try for one of those corporate jobs my students had, I was told the only way to get in the door with my dream company was to start in the call center. I went for it—and ended up writing speeches for the CEO and other executives and even going to the Olympics to work at a pop-up radio station on the slopes.

If it's flipping hamburgers at McDonald's, be the best hamburger flipper in the world. Whatever it is you do, you have to master your craft.

-Snoop Dogg

P.S. I did work at McDonald's, and was proudly the store's first female Quarter Pounder grill flipper.

FIVE USEFUL LESSONS FROM THE JERKS

I've been telling myself more and more that I never want to work with jerks again. It's a simple rule, but it saves a lot of headaches. It's amazing what money and power can do to people—how they're willing to throw respect and enjoyment out the window to get ahead.

Take this one time, for example. I worked with an obscure politician who fancied himself a hotshot entrepreneur. His wife was Romanian, and her best friend owned a pretty successful IT company looking to expand into Europe. Our politician friend took a stake in the company, started burning through cash, changed the company's name, and rented an over-the-top office in an expensive area.

The problem? He had zero management skills and no real connection with the people back in Romania. They didn't laugh at him outright, but they were clearly uneasy, knowing he had a stake in the company and ties to the founder.

When I first met him, I could feel the negative energy immediately, but I made the mistake of ignoring my gut. I felt sorry for the guy and wanted to help. After months of increasingly unpleasant interactions, we decided to part ways. I told him I wouldn't claim the shares he'd promised and moved on to my next assignment.

But then, out of nowhere, he went on the attack. Suddenly, everything was my fault, and he demanded an outrageous sum. He even enlisted the help of a shady character who had fled abroad due to fraud accusations. They both went after me hard. Legally, they didn't have a leg to stand on, and I had no interest in stooping to their level. I wished them luck and let them keep their pennies.

Lesson 1: *Trust Your Instincts.* When you sense negative energy, listen to your gut. Walking away early is better than getting entangled in someone else's drama.

Standing Your Ground

Then another time, I got summoned by the Dutch Country Manager of a large international IT service provider. This guy had a serious grudge against me: I was handling his biggest client and reporting directly to a VP in the US instead of to him. He decided I should make a "deal" with this client over some licenses. I refused. The deal was only worth 5 million euros, and at that moment, I was negotiating an extension worth nearly 300 million with the same client. Pushing his short-term agenda would have jeopardized our entire negotiating position and could have cost us way more than we'd gain.

When I laid out my reasoning, he got furious—stood up, shouted, and demanded to know who I thought I was. My calm response? "The one who's in charge." He completely lost it, and our relationship never recovered. The man just couldn't handle someone standing their ground.

Lesson 2: *Stand Firm on What Matters.* Don't let others push you into short-term decisions that could compromise long-term goals. Protect your position, even if it means ruffling a few feathers.

The Shortlist Gamble

When I started working in India, I had a chance to pitch to someone from the Board of Directors of a company I had done business with—a guy named Theo. He welcomed me warmly, shared his plans, and discussed my new employer. He was impressed but also mentioned that I was too late. They'd already researched India's market and selected the top three companies for a shortlist.

Unfortunately, we weren't on it.

I told Theo there must be a misunderstanding; according to my information, we were number two. I asked him to reconsider the shortlist. Theo called in someone from his staff, explained the situation, and then leaned back in his chair. "Edwin," he said, "we'll wait here for the outcome. If you're right, you'll be on the shortlist immediately. If not, you're not trustworthy, and we'll never see each other again."

Fair, but tough. I sweated bullets for an hour and a half until the assistant returned and confirmed I was right. Theo stood up, took me to his CIO, and introduced me: "This is Edwin; he's now on the shortlist." Theo became a client again, and an average of 500 people from India worked for his company for the next ten years. It was a nerve-wracking hour, but definitely worth it.

Lesson 3: *Back Yourself Up.* When you know you're right, don't be afraid to push for what you deserve. Just make sure you've got the facts to back it up.

After years of loyal service and significant successes, I got an email from the overseas headquarters. A major restructuring was coming, and it would affect everyone. Even my team was reorganized, and I had to let go of four people. These people had been key to almost all of my successes—absolute stars I could always count on. I lost sleep over it for days because these were the people who had supported me through thick and thin. I fought back, protested, and suggested alternative names—nothing worked.

In the end, I decided to resign. I believe in standing up for your principles, even if it means taking a hit or missing out on opportunities. People with principles know the feeling of loneliness I experienced during that time. But being able to look at yourself in the mirror and know you did the right thing? That's worth more than anything else.

Lesson 4: *Stick to Your Principles.* No job or paycheck is worth compromising your values. Sometimes, walking away is the best thing you can do.

The Handshake Deal

I once struck a deal with the owner of an IT company—just a few sentences exchanged, and we had a plan. He'd been running a successful organization for over a decade but had never broken through a revenue ceiling. He'd gone through three sales managers in recent years and was starting to realize that maybe it wasn't entirely their fault. He couldn't offer a high salary, but he was looking for a shared risk/reward setup with me as his prospective Chief Commercial Officer. The idea was to gain a stake in the company and share in the success we both hoped for. We agreed on a long-term partnership and shook hands.

After about ten months, we were still so enthusiastic that we reaffirmed the deal with another handshake. It was time to put things on paper, but that's a big step. He asked me, "How can you collaborate with me and take on some risk?" I had just one question: "For what amount would you sell your company right now, with no conditions?"

After some thought, he said, "100 million." I came up with a plan on the spot: "Give me 1% of whatever you sell it for above that 100 million, and we have a deal." It was as win/win as it gets, and he agreed. We planned to wait until one of the shareholders exited before putting it all in writing, thinking it would be easier to get everything right in one go. We shook hands again, and that was that—everything was cool. Or so I thought.

You guessed it: the company was sold for an enormous amount, well above the $100 million, and once the dust settled, I invited the founder—now a new multi-millionaire—for breakfast to discuss my next steps. With a straight face, my cheerful friend claimed he couldn't remember the deal we made and didn't want to talk about it anymore. He was sorry, he said, that "everyone wanted something from him now."

But he assured me I'd be the CCO of the new company. How that process unfolded is a story for later, but a few weeks after that promise, I met the new CEO, who told me, with a straight face, that she was going to fire me. Her legendary reason: "You're successful and charismatic, so I can never shine next to you." It wasn't just me; the rest of the management team was told they'd only receive two months' salary as a bonus. It stung, especially since they were all being removed or fired.

People often ask me if I was angry. My answer has always been the same: "Yes, at myself. I made the mistake of not putting agreements in writing immediately, assuming everyone thinks like I do—that a deal is a deal, and money isn't the most important thing."

Lesson 5: *Get It in Writing.* Handshake deals are great until they're not. Always put agreements in writing, no matter how trustworthy someone seems.

And as for the real jerks? My advice: avoid them whenever possible. Life's too short to waste on people who don't respect you.

FACING (OR FRONTING) THE FIRING SQUAD

Firing people is never easy—it gives almost everyone a terrible feeling. Almost everyone. An exception was an old classmate of mine, now a board member of a large insurance company. I ran into him by chance and complimented him on his impressive position and responsibility. I was somewhat surprised because he had never struck me as a high flyer.

When I asked him his secret, the answer was painful: "If a department needs to be closed or there's a mass layoff, they call me. I'm one of the few who enjoys doing it, and that's how I keep getting nice promotions." Ouch. If you're not built like this guy (congratulations), here are a few tips I've come to appreciate:

1. **The First Cut is the Deepest:** Tell the employee openly and honestly what's going on. It saves a lot of gossip and grief. By sitting down quickly, you save months of harassment and building cases. This way, the damage for both employee and employer is smaller, the employee can focus on finding a new job, and you might be able to have a beer together later ("It wasn't fun, but it was fair and decent, thank you.").

2. **Explain Why:** Try to explain satisfactorily why it's not working this time and here. Constructive criticism helps both parties improve and reduces the chances of it going wrong again.

3. **Negotiate with Respect:** In a good negotiation, both parties compromise. If there's a winner, there's also a loser. It's better to keep expectations realistic and meet somewhere in the middle. If there's mutual respect, a negotiation feels like a Martial Arts Kata—a form exercise, a dance.

4. **Legal Support is Advisory:** Good legal support helps you know what you are or aren't entitled to. But I see lawyers ideally as very valuable advisors: they help, but it's my decision and negotiation.

5. **If You Get Fired:** Remember one thing: the real solution is a new job. Focus your energy on finding it. Forgive, forget, and learn.

Every experience, whether positive or negative, offers a learning opportunity. Reflect on your journey, identify areas for improvement, and apply those lessons to future endeavors.

Remember: chances are, you've been here before and survived.

WALK THAT VERY THIN LINE

Carlos, my colleague and the bid manager for a big deal we had been working on together, burst into my office that morning and asked how I was feeling.

After all, today was the day we'd get the long-awaited call: after a year and a half of answering questions, making proposals, giving presentations, and having dozens of meetings, we would finally hear from the client.

The nearly $100-million deal would either be ours or go to our sole remaining competitor.

I gave a standard, superficial answer, and we joked around to ease the nerves, wishing each other luck. But as Carlos was about to leave, we both realized this reaction was inadequate. The mood shifted to a slightly more philosophical reflection. I asked Carlos what he thought about how we had worked as a team over the past 14 months.

Carlos said what I already knew: the team was fantastic, the atmosphere was great, our proposal was the best, and our relationship with the prospect had gone from zero to a hundred in that time.

And yet, there was still a competitor. I was sure our competitor felt the same way—they were also a respectable firm with very skilled employees who had worked passionately together. Soon, there would be a call with good news for one of us and bad news for the other. Carlos and I looked at each other and concluded that we were proud of our efforts, but our success would ultimately be determined by the outcome of that call.

A few hours later, the call came, and we were the lucky winners. I was sitting with my direct manager, discussing my performance, and suddenly I was handed a fantastic negotiating position. Everyone was thrilled; there was champagne in all the offices, and the team was celebrated for delivering a brilliant performance.

That was true, but what if the outcome had been different? What would have been the consequences for our competitor's team?

Amid the celebrating colleagues, Carlos and I exchanged a look that instantly reminded us of the thin line between everything and nothing. Strangely enough, that celebration marked a turning point in how I viewed success. I could finally put things into perspective—an ultimate buzzkill for any form of excess.

Years later, I had an informal lunch with Bert, the now-retired CEO of this client, and I asked him why they had chosen us and how large our lead had been.

Bert looked at me and warned, "You're not going to like this, Edwin." But he continued anyway: "During the evaluation, there were five board members, and we took a vote. It was immediately 2 for you and 2 for the competitor. The fifth person stared into space for almost a minute, repeating the names of both companies with a sigh after each name. He kept asking if he really had to choose, and only when the rest of the team pressured him to decide, did he give a big sigh and then said your name. I asked 'Why?' and he said, 'Both are fine companies, but we can only choose one.'"

That day, we won the deal; I got a promotion, a better salary, and a bigger bonus. I received an invitation to the Inner Circle, and everyone wanted to work with me on the next deal. Was it brilliant salesmanship? Brilliant strategy? Maybe. But it was also just enough to make it to the final two.

The difference between first and second place, between everything and nothing, is thin—paper-thin. Never forget that, and stay humble.

Learnings from the line

Celebrate Effort, Not Just Results: While winning is important, take pride in the hard work and teamwork that got you there. Success is often a result of collective effort, not just the final outcome.

Stay Humble: No matter how skilled or prepared you are, remember that outcomes can hinge on factors beyond your control. Recognize the thin line between success and failure, and maintain humility.

Perspective is Key: Use both victories and losses to gain perspective. Understand that sometimes, the difference between winning and losing can be a single decision made in a moment of uncertainty.

Always Prepare for the Unexpected: Just because you've done everything right doesn't guarantee a win. Prepare for all outcomes and learn from each experience.

Recognize the Role of Luck: Luck and timing can play a significant role in any success. Don't let it diminish your efforts, but do acknowledge it and stay grounded.

Embrace Innovation: Seeing Potential Where Others Don't.

Back in the 1990, I was in India, where it wasn't uncommon for employees to bring their older kids—around twelve years old—to the office on Saturdays. It created a relaxed atmosphere, and the kids got a firsthand look at what their parents did, often sparking their own interest in the work.

One Saturday, I noticed a man who had set up a makeshift table cluttered with chips and small devices. His son was helping him, and my curiosity got the better of me. I asked what they were working on, and he explained that it was a prototype for sending photos via mobile phones. The table was a chaotic mess of chips and wires, a far cry from the sleek gadgets we use today.

I remember thinking, "Why would anyone want to send photos with their phone? That seems really dumb." I dismissed his idea as a waste of time and moved on without giving it a second thought.

A few weeks later, it hit me—the potential of his invention. This was before the iPhone, in the early '90s—maybe 1992 or 1993. The guy eventually consolidated his setup into a single chip and offered it to Motorola, making him one of the pioneers of mobile photo sharing.

Looking back, I realized how my arrogance had blinded me to the innovation right in front of me. It wasn't the first time I'd seen something new and failed to grasp its potential. The internet, virtual insurance, the cloud, and now AI—I've met each with skepticism at some point.

This experience taught me a crucial lesson: just because I don't understand something doesn't mean it's worthless. Innovators look beyond the flaws and see what's possible. They see potential where others see impossibility.

Today, things like storing money on our phones and making wireless transactions are second nature. But it wasn't that long ago that people worried about someone walking by and making unauthorized transactions just by being near your phone. Focusing on those rare exceptions often blinds us to the broader potential of new technology.

I've come to deeply respect innovators who push the boundaries of what can be done. They remind us that progress comes from looking beyond what we know and daring to imagine what could be.

TRY THIS: Flex Your Innovation Muscles

These exercises work well with people from all sorts of roles and industries—especially those who don't typically see themselves as "creative."

- **"Stupid Idea" Makeover:** Think of an idea you once dismissed as "stupid" that actually turned out to be a big success. Now, take a current "stupid idea" and give it a makeover! How could you flip it into something brilliant?

- **Future Needs Forecast:** Take a wild guess—what will people need 20 years from now? Dream up three future needs, and then sketch out or describe inventions that could meet them. Don't hold back—go as futuristic as you can!

- **Everyday Object Reinvention:** Pick an everyday object, like a coffee mug or a paperclip. Now, let your imagination run wild—how could you reinvent it to solve a completely different problem or serve an unexpected purpose?

- **Tech Mash-Up:** Grab two random technologies—say, virtual reality and smart refrigerators. How could you mash them together to create something totally new and useful?

- **Constraint Creativity:** Choose a current technology, but here's the twist: slap a big limit on it (e.g., no electricity, has to work underwater). How would you reimagine or adapt it?

You never know—what starts as a lighthearted brainstorming session could lead to your next big breakthrough.

Bonus: Try something new, something you've never done before, and revel in being very, very bad at it. It's a fast track out of your comfort zone and can turn out to be a bravery booster.

GROWTH HURTS. DO IT ANYWAY.

In the first months of parenting my sons, I often turned to the classic book *Oei, ik Groei!* (English version: The Wonder Weeks) by Hetty van de Rijt and Frans Plooij, later editions with contributions from their daughter, Xaviera Plas-Plooi.

Progress, they point out, is signaled by crying, clinging, and crankiness.

Put another way, Growth=Change=Pain.

With rapid development comes resistance, and this doesn't go away as we get beyond the nursery. On the way to moving forward, you will be passing through those awkward, uncomfortable phases where resistance is strong - not unlike the 'terrible twos.'

I've seen this happen with someone full of potential—super talented, ambitious, and driven. I encouraged her to keep climbing, recognizing and suggesting that she could take over my role one day. But, as soon as I left the company, she retreated to a position she had outgrown years before, preferring the safety of the familiar over the risks that come with growth.

And that may be fine - if that's what you want. I hope by now you've realized that neither I nor this book have any intention of playing the role of a Guru, Method, or Teacher (as the legendary Van Morrison titled his brilliant album.)

I do highly recommend pushing through the fear and the expectations of others and asking the big question - What do I really want?   Then, get to the core and find your own compass.

Business schools around the world teach "root cause analysis," often drawing on the 5 Why Method created by inventor Sakichi Toyoda. When a problem occurs, ask "why" five times to try to find the source, then put into place something to prevent it from recurring. I've found it's a great way to draw a line between what you think you want or have been told you should want and what you really, at your core want to create.

Because, not much in life is certain, but these three things are: you will get taxed, you won't close all your deals, and you will die.

Do you feel good now? Actually...it's kind of freeing.

Having gone through a whole range of career bests and personal worsts, I've gotten better at making my own mix of what's important: family, health, friendships, sharing, and yes, working.

I could not have done it or continue to do it without the people who have helped, supported and inspired me along the way, interestingly often at just the right time.

These are the gurus, and they are all around you if you're paying attention.

Shiv Nadar's story? It's one that sticks with you. Here's a gentleman who built HCL from the ground up in India and then, instead of just resting on his piles of cash, decided to roll up his sleeves and change the game for education in his country. Early on, Shiv had the foresight to bring in a bunch of sharp executives to run the show at HCL.

That move gave him the freedom to chase his real dream: making sure the next generation of Indian kids had a fighting chance at a better life. Through his foundation, he bought up acres of rural land, threw up schools, built homes, and gave families a reason to send their kids to class. And, of course, when those kids graduated, there was always a spot waiting for them at HCL. Smart, right?

But here's the thing: It's not just the big players like Shiv who get my respect. Think about the young man who takes his disabled neighbor out for a walk. Or the woman who offers a kind word to the guy whose life has just gone to hell. These are the real heroes—the ones who know when enough is enough and decide to look out for the little guy.

As for me, I'm still grateful every single day for the lessons I learned from my youngest son, Aaron. His life, and even the years after, have been my greatest teachers. When we found out Aaron was disabled, my family and I spent almost a year fighting to find him the right school. We had to pack up and move to another city just to get him into a day care facility. That meant daily runs—dropping him off, picking him up.

And let me tell you, those drives were everything. I made it a point to be the one behind the wheel whenever I could. The ride there was a chance to reconnect, to get in sync with his autistic rhythms, to feel that pure, unfiltered joy of just being with him. Switching gears from work mode to connecting with an autistic child is no easy feat. But when it worked—when I'd get a smile, a soft touch, or even a quick hug—man, those moments were priceless.

If there's one thing that opens your eyes, it's spending a few hours with people for whom health is a luxury, not a given.

I'm telling you, your priorities change real fast when you see just how much good you can do for someone who really needs it.

This book? It's one of my small contributions. Something I would've liked to have read when I was in my twenties, hungry for some real talk from people who'd been around the block.

If this book puts a smile on your face, makes you feel like you can tap me on the shoulder for advice or an idea—then it's done its job. I'm here to help where I can.

Small Kindnesses

by Danusha Laméris

I've been thinking about the way, when you walk

down a crowded aisle, people pull in their legs

to let you by. Or how strangers still say "bless you"

when someone sneezes, a leftover

from the Bubonic plague. "Don't die," we are saying.

And sometimes, when you spill lemons

from your grocery bag, someone else will help you

pick them up. Mostly, we don't want to harm each other.

We want to be handed our cup of coffee hot,

and to say thank you to the person handing it. To smile

at them and for them to smile back. For the waitress

to call us honey when she sets down the bowl of clam chowder,

and for the driver in the red pick-up truck to let us pass.

We have so little of each other, now. So far

from tribe and fire. Only these brief moments of exchange.

What if they are the true dwelling of the holy, these

fleeting temples we make together when we say, "Here,

have my seat," "Go ahead—you first," "I like your hat."

BIG DEALS, BOLD GROWTH:

OUR A-Z INSPIRATION PLAYLIST AND READING LIST

playlist	reading list
A "Ain't Nobody" Rufus and Chaka Khan	The Asterix series by René Goscinny, Albert Uderzo
B "Black Cat Bone" Albert Collins, Robert Cray, Johnny Copeland	Born to Run by Bruce Springsteen
C "Countdown" Beyoncé	The Artist's Way by Julia Cameron
D "Don't Stop Believin'" Journey	DeDikkeVanDam by Johannes Van Dam
E "Elevation" U2	The Complete Poems by Emily Dickinson
F "Fast Car" Tracy Chapman	Surely You're Joking, Mr. Feynman by Richard Feynman
G "We Go Back" Buddy Guy & Mavis Staples	The Goldfinch by Donna Tartt

	Song	Book
H	"Hannah Jane" Hootie & The Blow Fish	The Art of Fielding by Chad Harbach
I	"I've Been to Memphis" Lyle Lovett	The Wisdom for Creating Happiness and Peace by Daisaku Ikeda
J	"Gallows Pole" Jimmy Page & Robert Plant	Jan Cremer (I, Jan Cremer) Jan Cremer
K	"Here Comes the Hot Stepper" Ini Kamoze	Shoe Dog by Phil Knight
L	"L'amour est un oiseau rebelle" Maria Callas	The Life in Lyrics by Johnny Cash
M	"Tennessee Whiskey" Morgan & Chris Stapleton	The Midnight Library by Matt Haig
N	" Your Own Sweet Way" The Notting Hillbillies	Night by Elie Wiesel
O	"Once Upon A Time in The West" Dire Straits	Outliers: The Story of Success by Malcolm Gladwell
P	Paganini's Violin Concerto No. 1 performed by Jaap van Zweden	Songteller: My Life in Lyrics by Dolly Parton
Q	"These Are The Days of Our Lives" Queen	Queen's Gambit by Walter Tevis

R	"It Doesn't Matter Anymore" Linda Ronstadt	Revolution From Within by Gloria Steinem
S	"Still the Same" Bob Seger	The Art of War by Sun Tzu
T	"That's the Way (I Like It)" KC and the Sunshine Band	Happiness Becomes You by Tina Turner
U	"Utereg me stadje" Herman Berkien	Unbroken by Laura Hillenbrand
V	"And the Cradle Will Rock" Van Halen	De Verloren Sleutels van de Vrijmetselarij by Manly P. Hall
W	"Willin'" Little Feat	Start with Why by Simon Sinek
X	Xmas Songs Elvis Presley	X-Ray: The Unauthorized Autobiography by Ray Davies
Y	"You Gotta Be" Des'ree	Year of Yes by Shonda Rhimes
Z	"Zydeco Man" Clifton Chernier	The Art of Possibility by Rosamund Stone Zander and Benjamin Zander

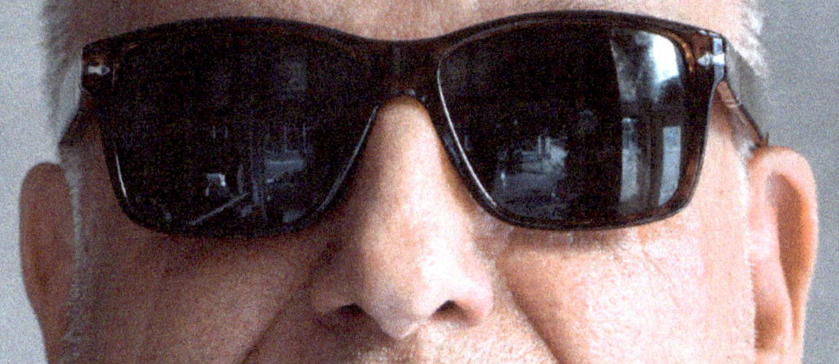

I don't know what to really say

Either we heal as a team
or we are going to crumble.
Inch by inch play by play
till we're finished.
We can stay here and get the
shit kicked out of us or we can
fight our way back into the
light.

One inch, at a time.
Because in either game,life
or football the margin for error
is so small.
I mean one half step too late
or to early, you don't quite
make it.
One half second too slow or
too fast, and you don't quite
catch it.

The inches we need are
everywhere around us.
They are in every break of the
game, every minute, every
second.

On this team, we fight for
that inch.
We CLAW with our fingernails
for that inch.

Cause we know when we add
up all those inches, that's going
to make the fucking difference
between WINNING and LOSING,
between LIVING and DYING

I'll tell you this, in any fight
It is the person who is willing
to die, who is going to win
that inch.
Because that is what LIVING is.
The six inches in front of your
face.

Now I can't make you do it.
But look into those eyes.
You are going to see one who
will go that inch with you.
You are going to see one who
will sacrifice for this team
Because when it comes down
to it, you are gonna do the
same thing.

That's a team.
And either we heal now,
as a team, or we will die as
individuals.

That's it, that's all it is.

Now whatta ya gonna do?

SalesPulse
Value
Selling
DON'T DECREASE THE GOAL,
INCREASE THE EFFORT.

Why SalesPulse Value Selling

- This SVS process addresses SalesPulse's organizational facing aspects of the bid. It is a handbook combining the available guidelines, processes and tools and pointing to relevant material available.

- To increase the quality and effectiveness of our proposals, we need to...

  - a strong client relationship, which should (ideally) be established before the proposal

  - Retain a sales perspective and rely on the sales individuals to own proposal and help to discover the winningsolution, pricing and timing

  - Have efficient and timely communication between departments, to ensure that the highest quality of proposal and delivery is achieved

  - Rely heavily on good knowledge of the sector, account and competitive landscapes

Objectives SalesPulse Value Selling

- Stop bidding on those we can't win
- Increase proposal quality
- Create a compelling value proposition
- Improve Knowledge Capture & Re-use

Increase the Win Rate

Improve bid resourcing

- Recognize the different skills and knowledge required on a bid
- Manage the availability of appropriate skills and resources

Healthy bid effort vs reward

- Provide a simple]process that people see value in using –SVS
- Get clear roles, responsibilities and bid timelines

increase funnel hygiene

- Obtain more accurate insights into funnel via Dynamics
- Get early warning of bids expected to come in

SalesPulse

We have established windesk to boost professionalism of the proposal process and increase the winrate

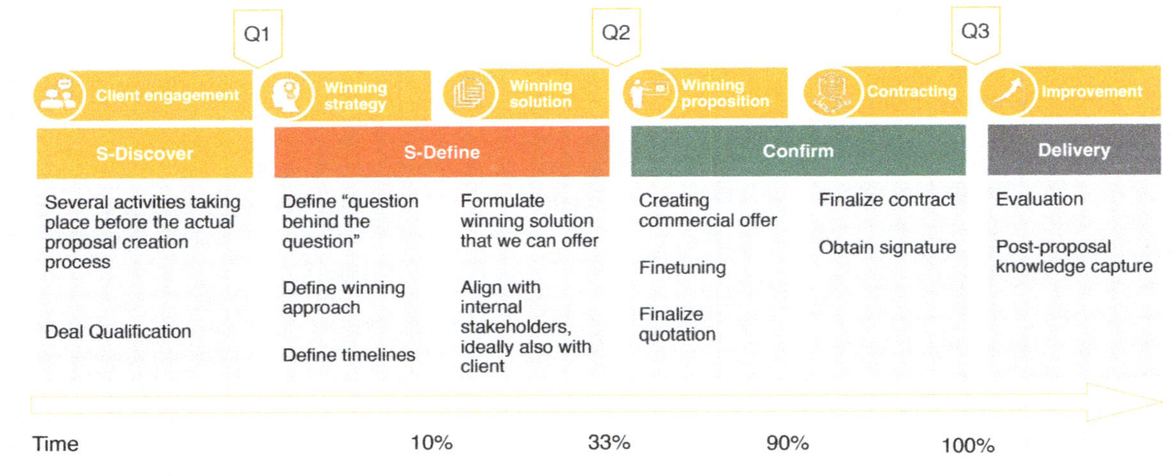

SalesPulse

Definitions

SalesPulse Value Selling (SVS): A process designed to bring guidance to a deal lifecycle and to ensure a smooth transition from commerce into operations, and to ensure that the "winning" team is involved in each phase

Windesk: The sales process enabler. Organizes the SVS-review board and runs the organizational aspects of proposals. Moreover, it supports in knowledge capture and deal review

SVS-review board: Helps each opportunity to switch to the next phase in the process. Has a focus on increasing the win chance and closing acceleration. The discussed content and participants depend on both the size andphase of the deal.

SalesPulse

While striving for Active References SalesPulse Value Selling (SVS) is our way of working

Sales Discover
COMMERCE

Sales indiv. in the lead

- Who do we need to speak with?
- What do we need to understand?
- Is the sense of potential correct?

Deliver
OPERATIONS

Sales indiv. hands over to Ops, stays in touch

- How is value best delivered?
- Sales indiv. stays close, to see if new/ cross-sell opportunities arise

Sales Define
COMMERCE + SOLUTIONS (+ PMO)

Sales indiv. in the lead, working with solutions

- Can we pin-point the potential?
- What is it exactly that the client needs?
- Where can we best help?

Confirm[1]
COMMERCE + SOLUTIONS[2] + PMO[1]

Sales indiv. in the lead, working with "virtual team"

- How do we prove potential value?
- Define proposal together with Ops, ideally involve Proj. Mngr.
- Present finished proposal

= WINDESK INVOLVEMENT

1: In confirm phase via PMO to OPS & Consulting,
2: Solutions is a mix from "commercial solutions" and CTO/ consulting experts

SalesPulse

Why discover

- During this phase we identify the right opportunities in order to select which ones to pursue
  - We are mainly looking for understanding:

- do we know enough to build the case for sales investments to be done?

- Are these deals of high potential in terms of revenue and win-probability?

"Saying no is one of the hardest things in sales and in business."

- An effective discovery phase enables you to qualify opportunities effectively.
  - This requires that your lead generation must be effective, to enable you to pick and choose the right opportunities;

- If we can say NO it means we did our Discover thoroughly and we will have better opportunities to pursue.

- Only by following Discover systematically, you can ensure we pursue only the right opportunities for SalesPulse

SalesPulse

Phase 1: Sales Discover

What needs to happen in this phase	**What are the questions to be answered before going to the next phase?**
• Establish/ maintain client relationships	• Why do we want the customer?
• Sales Individual contacts (ex-) customers and prospects, to gauge whether there is deal potential	• Why do we want the deal?
• Existing business ○ Potential deals can be spotted outside of commerce (Everyone's a salesperson)	• What is the "plan of attack", how are we going to win the deal?
• New business ○ Other departments are usually not involved in this phase	• Who are the competitors, and why is our proposition more interesting than theirs? • What are we going to offer? • What kind of resources will you need to fulfill the Sales-Define phase? • What will be the approximate scale of offering (Hours/ Revenue)?

SalesPulse

Why define

- Ensure that there is a clear understanding of the underlying client question. The question behind the question

- Ensure that there is an agreed solution before starting to develop the actual proposal

- Agreeing upon a clear action plan for the confirm phase. This to ensure that a winning approach is being taken and the win-rate is maximized.

- Define: In this phase you actually create and start executing your winning strategy and solution. To do so, it isimportant you could capitalize on the relationship work done earlier (in Discover). DIFFERENTIATION fromvcompetition and ALIGNMENT of all appropriate SalesPulse resources is key in this phase

SalesPulse

Phase 2: Sales Define

What needs to happen in this phase

- Identify who is the key decision maker, how will we get these "on our side" (extension from activities in Discover)

- Determine what the client is looking for exactly, in terms of products/ services/desired outcomes
  - What is the "question behind the question"

- Work on initial technical scoping of the client's request

- Formulate a winning sales strategy and winning solution

What are the questions to be answered before going to the next phase

- What is the "Question behind the question"?

- What is the solution that we are going to offer?

- Which delivery teams are going to be needed?

- Who else is needed from SalesPulse to form the winning bid team?

- What will the proposal deadline look like (BAFO date, presentations, check-points, etc.)?
  - Who needs to be involved at what stage

Additional steps in case of complex deal

- Who will be in the Proposal team? (SDM, Consultant, Expert, PM, etc.)

- When is which SalesPulse consultant going to the client for co-creation or a workshop?

- When is which SalesPulse Senior exec. going to the client?

- Before going into qualification, conduct a "solution review", is the proposed solution the best that we can do?

Why confirm

- The confirm phase is ensures that the winning strategy and sales plan are finalized

- In Confirm we must convey our solution to our client in a way they perceive their needs are recognized and catered for. Our proposal (whether it is a presentation, a compilation of written plans or simple pitch) needs to have the right content and at the same time look nice, plus have consistency. A proposal should be presented by SalesPulsens that are enabled to do so and after a proper sign off at the right level.

SalesPulse

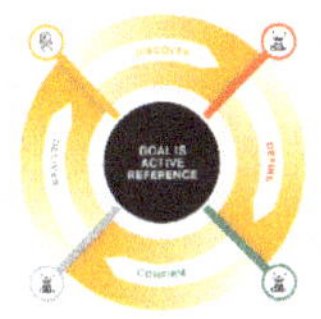

Phase 3: Confirm

What needs to happen in this phase	What are the questions to be answered before going to the next phase

What needs to happen in this phase

- Write a winning proposal
  - Collaboration between Commerce and Consulting and Operations where needed
- Align on exact proposed solution/ timelines/ necessary resources for delivery
- Proper mapping of the risks and liabilities of the proposed solution
- Proposal is offered to the client (proposal confirm)
- Negotiations are completed
- Final signature is obtained

What are the questions to be answered before going to the next phase

- Pre- signature overview, including the to-be signed papers & management summary
- Overview of:
  - Revenue
  - Margin
  - Risks
- What are the risks and liabilities?
- What exactly are we going to offer?
- What resources are needed from Ops/ Consulting?
- What is the proposed delivery date?
- Signature from the person with signing authority (Edwin, Ian, Rick, Dependent on deal-size)

SalesPulse

Phase 4: Deliver

- Handover from commerce to Operations and/ or consulting via PMO

- Post (tender) opportunity evaluation

- Knowledge capture

SalesPulse

The winning approach for 6 weeks of proposal production
(SVS stages S-Define and Confirm)

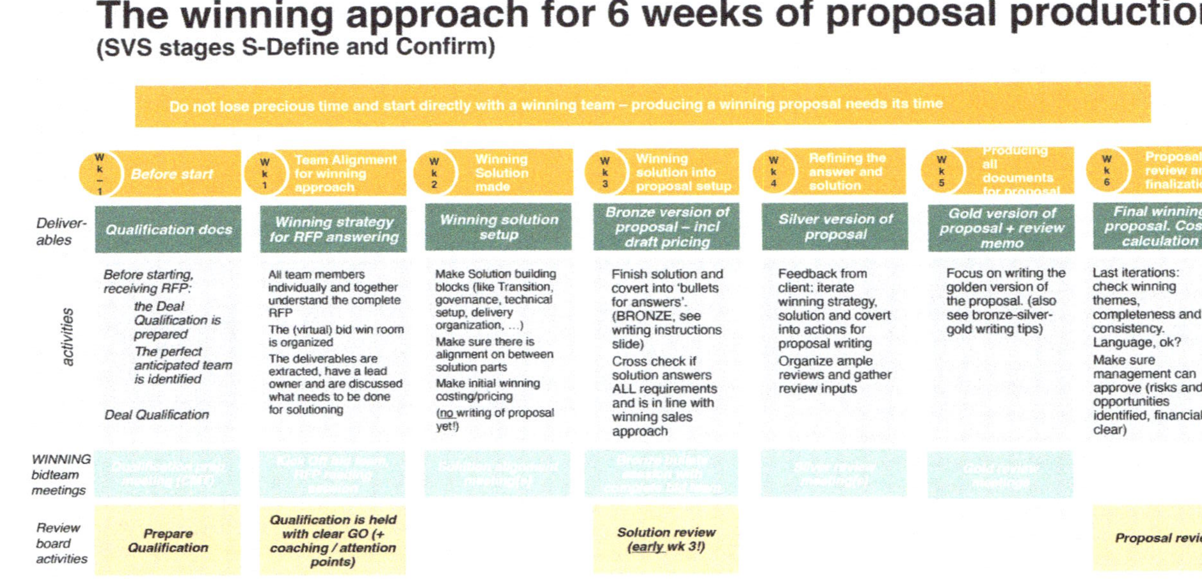

	Wk-1 — Before start	Wk1 — Team Alignment for winning approach	Wk2 — Winning Solution made	Wk3 — Winning solution into proposal setup	Wk4 — Refining the answer and solution	Wk5 — Producing all documents for proposal	Wk6 — Proposal review and finalization
Deliverables	Qualification docs	Winning strategy for RFP answering	Winning solution setup	Bronze version of proposal – incl draft pricing	Silver version of proposal	Gold version of proposal + review memo	Final winning proposal. Costs calculation
activities	Before starting, receiving RFP: the Deal Qualification is prepared. The perfect anticipated team is identified. Deal Qualification	All team members individually and together understand the complete RFP. The (virtual) bid win room is organized. The deliverables are extracted, have a lead owner and are discussed what needs to be done for solutioning	Make Solution building blocks (like Transition, governance, technical setup, delivery organization, …). Make sure there is alignment on between solution parts. Make initial winning costing/pricing (no writing of proposal yet!)	Finish solution and covert into 'bullets for answers'. (BRONZE, see writing instructions slide). Cross check if solution answers ALL requirements and is in line with winning sales approach	Feedback from client: iterate winning strategy, solution and covert into actions for proposal writing. Organize ample reviews and gather review inputs	Focus on writing the golden version of the proposal. (also see bronze-silver-gold writing tips)	Last iterations: check winning themes, completeness and consistency. Language, ok? Make sure management can approve (risks and opportunities identified, financials clear)
WINNING bidteam meetings	[illegible]	[illegible]	[illegible]	[illegible]	[illegible]	[illegible]	
Review board activities	Prepare Qualification	Qualification is held with clear GO (+ coaching / attention points)		Solution review (early wk 3!)			Proposal review

SalesPulse

EXTRAS & RESOURCES

LinkedIn
https://www.linkedin.com/in/edwinkennedy/
https://www.linkedin.com/in/kateyandohharris/

Contributors

Text and content	www.salespulse.nl
Design, art direction	www.sprklmarketing.nl
Photography	www.studiohuibvanwersch.com
Illustration	www.kommunikative.com.mx

Papageno: If you want to do some good with your money, consider donating to the amazing foundation run by Jaap and Aaltje van Zweden, Stichting Papageno. They're using the power of music to support kids and young people with autism.

https://www.papageno.nl/en/